Miracles of South Carolina

True Stories of Grace in the Palmetto State

Robbie Goodall Boman

I trust that these "heightened testimonies" of grace will lift your soul —

— In Christ,

Robbie

11-08

Shelor & Son Publishing, LLC

Psalm 136=4

ISBN 13: 978-0-9761460-1-8
ISBN 10: 0-9761460-1-0

Library of Congress Control Number: 2008930873

Cover photograph by Cliff and Liz Shelor
Author photograph by Josh Norris, copyright © 2007 by
The Greenville News
Cover design by Bill May and Stellar Studios

Shelor & Son Publishing, LLC
312 Fairmount Terrace
Mountville, PA 17554

www.SHELORandSON.com

1 2 3 4 5 6 7 8 9 0

To all who have gradually released their hold on the miraculous and watched it drift upward and away, soon to vanish entirely from sight . . .

To those who *can no longer believe* that such wondrous things really happen . . .

To these same fine people who maybe—just maybe—want that original trust back in their lives.

Contents

Preface

Thanks for reaching for this little volume, perhaps just out of curiosity. You may be interested in South Carolina, or in miracles, or in both.

I myself am merely a reporter of remarkable events and answered prayers. More of a reporter than an explainer, for who on earth can fully interpret miracles? You hold in your hands a small sample. More than half of these accounts are gleaned from the Upstate because that's where I live and know the most people. While compiling these chapters I have collected notes on additional miracles from the Judeo-Christian tradition, and those will keep nicely—should they be needed—tucked away in a journal for now. They wouldn't all crowd into this one place.

These are exciting times. Quiet surprises as well as over-the-top events are happening in everyday lives across the Palmetto State and elsewhere. Perhaps you have already noticed this. I have for years, but never thought to put the stories down on paper. Fortunately, Derik Shelor phoned me out of the blue and offered an opportunity to jump in and do just that. I see this as a chance to give form and substance to the intangible and unseen activities of God in my very own region. After initially turning down the assignment, I decided to follow my daughter's urging and try. This book is just that. A try.

Please set aside some time. Pore over these true tales and see what you think. Amazing memories from your own life may bubble up into consciousness as you do. Almost all of the stories in this book are told here publicly for the first time, and I appreciate folks' willingness to step out. It takes courage to do so. Sharing perhaps the most unusual moment of one's life is not easy, but is often beneficial. It can lift others' weary loads and infuse them with new hope and faith.

My primary target audience is skeptics. Yes, I am a Christian, deeply flawed but rather fervent. Most people featured in these pages are also Christians. If that bothers some readers, I'd suggest forging ahead anyway. Forgive that I'm not a great writer. Skip around and read a few chapters anyway before putting this book down, so as not to miss something significant. One episode may not appeal to the soul, but another might. And what if that very chapter is tucked away at the end of the book? As a former agnostic for twenty-six years, I'd recommend the willing suspension of disbelief just to hear these honest voices speak directly from personal, stark experience.

Each episode was gathered from friends or people who became friends while doing this project. It was a warm exchange. Carolina narratives flowed freely from open hearts. Often, and rather surprisingly, when the subject of miracles came up during my research, people rushed to speak; they seemed compelled to do so. When in a group, one person often interrupted another with full-throttle enthusiasm to tell a story first. This was not selfish zeal. Instead, it acknowledged a pent-up desire to find someone, *anyone,* who would really listen and not dismiss a supernatural occurrence as a lie or "crazy." That's the word people almost always used.

Wonders have been discussed and analyzed for thousands of years, and I will not attempt to do that now. But here are some points I have observed repeatedly—though not in every case—while working on the twenty-eight chapters. Most of these ideas surface in biblical teachings:

- Supernatural moments do change hearts and lives, once they are perceived and accepted. A humbling, genuine shift seems to take place in the personality. The people interviewed frequently mention this, as the lady called "Angel" demonstrates in the first chapter.
- Brenda's tiny key miracle in chapter 9 shows that extraordinary graces come in all sizes and shapes.
- Just about every Carolinian on record here thinks

about his or her special message often, even daily. It serves as a mysterious touchstone, question mark, or faith rock. (Gerrie, now back home and working in New York City, often refers to a vision of Jesus she had while living in Greenville. See chapter 7.)

- Contrary to some stereotypes, the divine interventions discovered in the writing of this book were intense but not sappy or silly. These magnified testimony events were not vague; neither were they simply ethereal. On the contrary, each interviewee described a super-charged slice of time in precise, objective, factual language. It seemed vital to translate the experience, to get it just right in understandable, precise, human terms. For instance, the warrior angel observed by an Episcopal clergyman in chapter 21 was suited up in breastplates, armor, and a helmet.

- Journaling is common. A dozen or more people in this book have written things down. They did so to keep the memories fresh and to prevent exaggeration later. "This was the single most incredible experience of my life," says a diarist in chapter 24.

- Almost every spiritual event shared by people from the Coastal area, Midlands, or Upstate unlocked a revelation or personal "call." Sometimes a brief instant affirmed a life direction already known, or re-energized a mission long buried and forgotten. For example, Lib in chapter 11 felt a mantle of "motherhood" descend when she accepted charge of her older brother in Orangeburg. He has Down syndrome, Alzheimer's, and Parkinson's disease.

- Across the board, from Charleston to Columbia to Greenville, no one lacked confidence. They knew they spoke facts. It didn't much matter if *others* believed—or didn't believe—a miracle tale. It didn't matter if others partly understood it, didn't know

ix

about it at all, or entirely supported the supernatural encounter. These events were self-authenticating—if somewhat mysterious—to the people who received them. Once someone saw an angel commanding over a kitchen, heard a Voice that averted a horrific accident, had a blind eye healed instantaneously, or lay near death during a huddled prayer meeting as cancer was eradicated head-to-toe—once these things occurred, there was simply no need for further human confirmation. *Something* had taken place. When truly at work, the Divine Hand stamps a soul authoritatively. "Miracle after miracle was happening" during mission trips to the Ukraine, says Johnnie in chapter 23.

Miracles of South Carolina was an enjoyable project, thanks to an unusually kind and skillful publisher. I also appreciate the guidance and long-suffering technical assistance of my husband, Harold, of thirty-two-plus years, who backs my ventures and adventures; the love and laughter of children James and Sally, now in their twenties; the encouragement of sister Lee and husband Jon, along with Caroline, Laura, and Grace; plus friends who prayed often for this particular endeavor. Some have stories recorded in a chapter. Others include Krista Bannister, Reverend Debora Bishop, Betsy Boyer, Kathleen Cull, Becky Fly, Reverend Bob Hall, Jennifer Hammond, Bette Hedden, Marie Newton, Margo Patton, Nancy Pavelka, Nancy Pennell, Reverend Deb Richardson-Moore, Gwynn K. Smith, and my "grandparents in Christ" Paul and Leta Poston, who published a South Carolina book first.

Finally, some dictionary sources confirm "smile" as an ancient root for "miracle." May you, too, smile as you read these stories of grace.

Miracles of South Carolina

Remarkable Moments at a Soup Kitchen Church
A Place Where God Shows Up

Whenever hurting people desperate for God and a free meal gather at an old brick church in downtown Greenville, the supernatural breaks out. It just does. The spiritual climate seems right—energized with belief and thick with deep need.

Amazing events erupt without warning. This happens among the homeless, the working poor, the addicted, the just-evicted, the day laborers, ex-cons, transients, people just laid off, and those of us blended across denominations and racial borders from forty-five churches who work with them. Sure enough, we too could be in their shoes. Ask anybody at the Triune Mercy Center, where for almost two decades sheer human kindness and the whispered possibility of "a miracle" has kept thousands alive with hope. First-time volunteers sometimes leave in tears.

Yes, the Divine really seems to show up at ministries like this—nitty-gritty meeting grounds where hunched people rub out their cigarettes with muddy boots before trudging inside for a dinner of ham, green beans, rolls, and potato salad handed out by a local church. Hopeless folks, sure, but also expectant. After all, who can say what God might do? When He might really, truly arrive with a personal word? A job? A drug-free room to sleep in? A tangible display of compassion or strength or deliverance? Who can say He won't? After all, most of them lived through the night without getting stabbed or shot, without freezing to death, didn't they? And that was a miracle, wasn't it?

Other than "work" or "shelter," the most popular prayer request on record at the Triune Mercy Center: "Thank you, Lord, for letting me see another day."

A Stranger Wanders Back "Home"

Consider the case of one needy African-American lady who drifted into the ministry in the spring of 2006. She hung around, waiting for whatever "helps" might be available: a bag lunch, a blanket, a hygiene pack, or maybe even some shoes. She was alone and sadly dressed, yet chatty and sweet. She flashed a personable smile from some deep repository of joy not yet drained dry. Shaky from any number of possible addictions, she hitched up with a volunteer quite naturally. I was sweeping through the center as always on Wednesdays, looking for people to pray for the City of Greenville in Triune's adjoining chapel. We have committed this hour, noon to 1 p.m., since April 2004.

"What's your name? Want a Bible? We've got them for free," I prodded as we rounded the sidewalk corner of Stone and Rutherford and took our time edging toward the sanctuary steps. "Angel," she said, establishing that we were already on miracle ground.

Was "Angel" a street name? Her real name? An imagining? What she greatly desired to be? Or what she in fact was?

Then came, "Yes, I want a Bible. I want a new start, I want to start over."

She was tired of being on drugs, too.

So, once the street dweller passed the threshold of the quiet, old sanctuary, a peaceful Angel appeared instead. She cast her eyes far, far up along the arched wooden beams and stained glass windows flanking us on every side. Awed, she remained silent as we walked the center aisle. We swept past long rows of pews toward an imposing but darkened stained glass window behind the pulpit. It required backlit illumination, so I flipped a switch. Instantly, light bathed Jesus in Gethsemane with painterly blues, reds, and gold.

Angel was home, truly at home in church.

"Come on in here. This is where the Bibles are kept," I urged. We headed back together into a dark, musty hall where hung robes, stoles, and a funny jumble of old, artificial flowers and Christmas decorations. "Here's a bunch of Bibles people gave us. I'll get you one."

She said nothing as I examined the first. Too tattered, I judged. The letters unbelievably small, hard to read, the whole thing falling apart. I sensed we could do much better. This lady deserved it. I reached for the next Bible, in better shape, but not much, easily twenty years old. Oh well, donations were low. Bibles came in from everywhere and we would have to put the word out again for more. I opened the front cover as she looked on. We stopped and saw it together.

Scrawled in large, penciled, capital letters across the front two empty pages were the words "Welcome Home, Angel."

Stunned, she said nothing. I didn't either. Then, "Clearly, Angel, this one's for you. God sure knows you and knows you are here. This is amazing. Take it."

Overcome with feeling, Angel hugged her precious cargo— truly marked as a God-autographed Bible—her head down, and headed back into the sanctuary. She dropped to her knees and sobbed muffled prayers and personal confessions before the altar for half an hour as I hurriedly shared the story with a delighted group of seven or so regular intercessors, now seated near the front. We had come together, as always, to pray for the city, state, nation, and world. And so we did.

Meanwhile, Angel had settled into her chosen spot. Feeling unworthy even to kneel on the altar cushions, she prayed on the floor the whole time, rising only to lift up the city's poor, and then to ask if she could sing Psalm 121, which she knew by heart. The tune was created right there on the spot. Surely she led the prayer service. It was a hymn of thanksgiving to a God

3

who, years ago, had used someone somewhere to pen His personal message of homecoming to her—and in His very own book, too.

I don't recall ever seeing this lovely lady before that day or after. Thousands come and go at Triune and around the city. People move in; people move out. Someone mentioned perhaps seeing her sheltered under a bridge at one point. Who knows? In fact, the name Angel applies to all those we may entertain unaware.

But I remember how that particular Angel's voice rang out strong and singular, no word misplaced. She clutched her Bible fiercely throughout a sacrifice of praise. After years of pain, she had irrefutable evidence that God really meant it when He said, "Welcome Home."

Mysterious Hero Rescues Girls from Dam's Edge

If a mysterious stranger had not stepped in to save them, the two girls in a canoe would have crashed over a spillway and fallen thirty feet to their deaths on the jagged rocks below. Laura Cross of Aiken remembers her daughter Lindsey's peril and rescue as if it were last week. It happened in the early 1990s, just before the Cross family moved from Colorado to South Carolina. "I believe it was an angel," Laura declares, a supernatural being sent by God to save her daughter and young friend from careening over the dam to the savage boulders and swirling water below.

Lindsey, now grown, married, and living in Ohio with children of her own at the time of the interview, was thinking back to that lake outing. "It was a beautiful day in the mountains of Colorado. The sky was clear and bright and blue."

After church they went canoeing at Lake Evergreen. Laura and her husband, Ben, often invited friends for outdoor activities on Sunday afternoons, and this time they brought an adult single friend. Eleven-year-old Lindsey asked a Sunday school girlfriend, age ten or eleven, to come along.

"The lake was very calm that day, just a gorgeous day," recalls Laura.

The parents felt confident that the girls could handle their own boat, since they had taken canoeing lessons at camp. The three adults set out in one canoe, while the girls took another, all in the same part of the lake.

"We convinced my parents to [let us] get in a canoe by our-selves. We started out staying really close together," says Lindsey, reconstructing the scene in her mind.

The Colorado mountains are ravishingly gorgeous, but they are also known for unpredictable weather. Without warning, dark storm clouds assaulted the snow-tipped peaks, then marched across the lake, showing no mercy for those in their path. "Storms [came] up in a moment," says Laura. "The water started getting real choppy."

The ominous wind swept both canoes in its path, especially the lighter one paddled by the girls. The adults' canoe was natu-rally heavier than the girls' boat, which began to blow rapidly away toward danger. In weather like this, the surly waves and wind were capable of pushing a light canoe right over the spill-way, onto the rocks and rapids below.

"Our two canoes started to separate and the wind began to carry my friend and me toward a dam at the opposite end of the lake," says Lindsey. "The dam wall, we had noted on our way in, was probably about thirty feet down with lots of sharp rocks at the bottom. The wall came only one foot over the wa-ter, and when the wind picked up, the water had no trouble going over it."

The situation was treacherous. The girls struggled against the forces of nature. Their paddles made little difference. All the while, the adults were hollering directions and warnings.

"My friend and I tried frantically to row away from the dam," says Lindsey. Her mom Laura adds, "We were trying to catch up with them."

This was the worst moment of Laura's life, and possibly the most deadly predicament that the two girls would ever face.

"I was just getting frantic," says Laura, "I was literally screaming out to God, 'Don't let them go over the dam!'"

Then, strangely enough, two men appeared precisely at this point, one after the other.

Lindsey notes, "We were about fifteen feet away from go-ing over and a man ran by us on the lakeside walkway." He was rather nondescript, a white man, not memorable except for one thing—he was angry. Instead of helping the girls, he cursed them. Laura remembers the same thing, recalling in astonishment, "He yelled, 'What are you trying to do, kill your [expletive, expletive] selves?'"

He yelled repeatedly, but did nothing to assist.

The girls glided by. Things were happening fast. They were now a mere ten feet from the spillway. Then Lindsey saw a second man appear. She remembers that he was a black man.

"When we were about ten or less feet from going over, a man came to the edge of the lake and calmly told us to try really hard to get to the side and he would hold us until my parents were able to make it over. . . . We made it to the edge and the man did as he said he would. My parents finally got there and one got in with me, the other with my friend.

"The strange thing was, when we looked up to thank the man, he was nowhere in sight. Here's the thing—it was impossible for him to disappear. There was nowhere for him to hide! I remember that story vividly to this day."

Lindsey recollects the mysterious stranger's face, his voice, "his kindness."

Her mother, Laura, never saw the man at all. She never saw anybody there to help. But her husband and daughter did, and she believes them.

Ben did not see the man's face, but tells this: "I remember seeing the man leaning over and holding the canoe till we got there. I stepped into the canoe with the girls and I remember the man stepping back one step and then he was gone."

Ben had turned to thank the hero, but he was not there. There was no hand to shake, no name to remember, no eyes to look into. "I never saw his face or saw where he went. There was really nowhere he could walk off to, out of sight quickly. Of course, my focus was on the safety of the girls, but I clearly remember how astonished I was that someone had quickly gotten to them to hold the canoe."

Ben continues, "I definitely thought we had no chance of getting to the girls before they got to the dam, but somehow this individual got them and held their canoe just feet from the dam."

Laura says, "I just felt like God heard our cries. He just took over and sent an angel. I wouldn't be convinced otherwise. It literally took me years before I could retell the story without reliving it, the terror of that day. It took years getting over that terror. They would have been dashed on those rocks. They got over it a lot quicker than I did."

Since then, Lindsey senses that God has had His hand on her life for some special purpose and has shielded her repeatedly. Her mother agrees, saying, "Maybe He has something for her to do, or maybe God has some special purpose for her children. There have been times when I felt like we have been watched over by angels. God sends people and we just don't realize it. God is so good. If we could see the many times He has protected us, we would be amazed. I believe when we get to heaven we will get to see."

Lindsey concurs: "I am a firm believer in miracles and angels. I have had many other [amazing] accounts that I can share if you like."

Author's note: Ben Cross, Ph.D., is a mechanical engineer, and Laura, a homemaker, holds a degree in business administration with an emphasis in accounting. Lindsey and her family have since moved to Aiken.

South Carolina Prayer Hits Arizona

On December 3, 2006, another quiet Triune Mercy Center miracle rippled across time and space, neatly demonstrating the force of corporate prayer. That night, while the congregation lifted to heaven one particular name and life, that same hometown girl—just days away from graduating from faraway Arizona State University—felt the impact.

That Sunday evening the congregation knit together as usual to sing, worship, hear preaching, and meditate over a rather long list of "prayers of the people." Typical soup kitchen pleas were that someone's lights be cut back on within the week, that a hospitalized man recover after being hit by a car, or that a woman find shelter until morning . . . the people's own stark, straight-up needs, to be sure. I had hurriedly jotted down about sixty entries during supper and afterward. The last few were compiled as some folks headed directly into the chapel, while others merged into the dark, uncertain streets and dirt paths leading from the Mercy Center.

A man or two always nodded away prayer because they felt too far gone for it to do any good. God wasn't listening, anyway, was He?

Candles lit, piano playing, the service began. Just before a pastor called for prayers, I impulsively pulled out Laura's graduation invitation. It seemed the thing to do. The Holy Spirit stirred. Tucked inside my Bible for over a week now, the Arizona State announcement engraved with a gold seal was a reminder of her years of hard work, a commencement less than a week ahead, and then plans for continued studies in graduate school.

I also grabbed the photo of a man in prison. His relative, a choir member, sat nearby and let me carry the photo to the front.

Now on my feet and at the podium, I reminded the group how Laura inspired others in daily life, how she and her guide dog, Jira, had volunteered at Triune any number of times, sometimes handing out tea to hundreds, at other times just smiling and talking with the people, or praying targeted needs at City Prayer. Although Laura first began losing her sight at age eight and now cannot see, she would soon graduate with honors and then attend seminary somewhere in the United States. (In my mind, I recalled her dressed in jeans and a pastel t-shirt, her blonde hair shining, engaging a crowd of Triune parishioners.)

So, in one hand I lifted up Laura's victory document. In the other, I held high the image of the smiling man up for parole soon. We hoped for success there, too. He attended inmate Bible study and worked inside the walls. These, I said, were special prayers before we began our intercessory list.

The next day I emailed Laura, a young woman who daily "walks by faith, not by sight." She connected the spiritual dots. She signaled back that those unknown spiritual petitions— prayed by church people that very night—had galvanized her already firm decision to apply to seminary and pursue a Master's degree in Christian counseling. She hopes to be a hospital chaplain.

My email read:

"We prayed for you by name at Triune last night. Over 100 there. The five-member (new!) praise band from The Salvation Army was there. Terrific. You would have loved it. Two guys your age in there and the rest, 'old rockers' now graduates of rehab, etc. I held up your graduation invitation, said you had been there [as a volunteer]. I explained how you are graduating with honors, courageously, far across the nation, without sight, but with a guide dog! How you plan a Master's degree and ministry in pastoral counseling; had prayed at Triune City Prayer, etc. Now, that invitation is returned to my Bible to inspire ME. Thanks! In Christ, Robbie."

Laura's response:

"Thank you, thank you, thank you! Wow! I am humbled and honored that I was lifted up last night at Triune. I am in awe of our perfect God! I desperately needed those prayers last night. I am praising God that he once again provided for my needs. Yesterday afternoon I was hit with horrible anxiety as I organized applications for seminary. I was able to somewhat claim scripture, but it wasn't until last night that I was able to stand firm in Christ and not give in to the anxiety. I know I was able to do that because of a direct result [of the prayers]. . . . Words can't express how grateful I am."

Several months later, Laura was accepted to Princeton Theological Seminary and received scholarships for the full amount of her first year's studies. She joined the campus in August of 2007 as the first blind student in the history of the seminary and began a chaplaincy internship at JFK Medical Center in the summer of 2008.

4

The Night I Was Healed

Before God restored Becky Rochester—ankle and soul—the Triune pianist first had to fall down flat at the church threshold (choir books, bag, and all) and then be lifted to a graceful stance by three strong men from the Mercy Center.

That warm September night in 2004 when Becky showed up limping for choir practice, no one suspected that she was not only physically injured but heartsick, too. No one would have believed it. Why, the sanctuary glowed whenever Becky arrived. Her effervescent personality and eruptions of laughter, her direct gaze and sincere listening ear—these always drew a crowd around the piano bench. Warm-up sessions generally started late because of the friendly commotion and rustling songbooks.

At the time of her church door accident, Becky was fairly new. Reverend Jerry Hill had just recruited her to help build a "mass choir" from two or three irregular attendees. Jerry, a popular gospel singer himself and a staff pastor at Buncombe St. United Methodist Church who often preaches at Triune on Sunday nights, teamed up well with the jazzy pianist.

"From the time I was three I've been singing in front of people," admits Becky, who has directed other local choirs and still does. The beaming redhead in her late fifties welcomes a microphone with fearless independence, yet points her finger to the heavens after every offertory to punctuate who gets real credit for her solos. This former Furman student, an ex-chain smoker/nightclub singer who rings out gospel like no one else—who could believe she dragged around an invisible anchor of grief?

12

And yet it was true. Becky was often sad. A reservoir of hurt had pitched and rolled deep inside since her mother's death of leukemia several years before. This daughter, joined by her elder sister and relatives, had maintained a bedside vigil at the old Blue Ridge country homestead right up until the end. Becky recalls, "Especially since I had been staying with her, when she died it was just this big void, this big hole in my life. And I went on antidepressants almost immediately and was not able to shake this grief."

Early in life, a series of tragic events had pelted the happy but hard-working family. Becky's farming father died when she was twenty-six. An elder sister followed soon afterward with cancer, leaving behind a husband and five children, the oldest only twelve. Alone with a remaining sister and her mom, Becky's own marriage dissolved: "I have no children. My marriage was not a happy one," she says quietly.

But as Providence would have it, an evening at church that began with a hurt ankle would emerge as a blessing. Becky would enter with private sorrow and walk out two hours later a radiant, refreshed woman, the glad recipient of two transformational healings—one physical and the other emotional.

How It Happened

A fall to the floor set things in motion. It was forty-five minutes before the 6 p.m. service and Becky was toting a load of music when she edged through the heavy oak chapel door. Soon her right foot caught. She fell sideways. Immediately, a young African-American lady from the Salvation Army group attending that night jumped to her aid. She offered, "Do you need me to call 911?"

No, it was okay, Becky assured her. She didn't want that much help. And yet, the foot was truly hurt, possibly fractured. "You can't get me up, I'm too big," Becky admitted to the woman, who summoned the aid of three guys nearby. "That would be the only way I could have gotten up. I say that in jest, but I'm a substantial woman," Becky observes, thinking back on the event.

There was another problem. Each Sunday after church, Becky worked third shift as a security monitor for the school district. As minutes passed, she became more and more concerned about the injured foot and also about her job later that night. "During the service it just got worse and worse, and I thought, 'Man, I bet I've chipped something in there, and I don't want to have to go to the emergency room between now and time to go to work, because I'll be late to work if I do.'"

Becky lasted through the hour. She sang and played as usual, her face narrowed in pain. Seeing this, after the service I asked if a group could lay hands on her and intercede. Spontaneously, about ten friends drew round this woman in need. A cross-section of humanity, it was—men and women, both homeless and suburbanites, of all ages and several nationalities, including a couple originally from Belfast, Northern Ireland, and a preacher from Africa.

The piano sat next to the sanctuary wall with a stained glass window behind. Becky grew still, her aching foot extended, eyes closed. She turned on the bench to face the altar and waited. All around, loving members of the congregation placed hands on her right shoulder, back, and arms.

"As many people as could had their hands on me. But there wasn't room for anybody to stand behind me," she recalls.

Her forehead and hands were anointed with oil fragrant with frankincense and myrrh. One pair of hands cradled her throbbing foot, touched with oil as well. Becky admitted later that, although she had prayed with others many times throughout her life—eyes shut, hands held tight—this was her first experience with anointed, hands-on prayer.

Her own words carry the next minutes.

"I had never had anybody do that before. But all I could think of was Jesus washing the disciples' feet. I thought, 'Nobody has ever knelt at my feet before.' It was a service picture. . . . The servant of Christ, is what I was thinking of. . . .

"This was a life-changer right there. Because when I think of anointing, I think of Samuel anointing David, and I think of being

14

anointed in readiness for ordination, I think of anointing special people for special events. I never had thought of it as ordinary people. So I was in that frame of mind. It was really strange.

"And while this was happening, I felt a heat in my foot, in my ankle. Not a burning. It was like a warmth. It was not painful. It was like a warm, soaking feeling. The only way I describe it is if you think of the way lava looks. It's just flowing, without the pain . . . just a liquid molten feeling inside my foot. It felt like two sides were going counter to each other, but you never felt the edges. Felt like shifting, two currents in a counter-clockwise direction, meeting. But there was no friction when they met. There was no 'splash' when they met. . . .

"And all of sudden, it was just like something slipped into place, like a gear. Not that angular, not that solid. It was just there was just a little empty place in a cup and all of a sudden, it got to where it could fill it up. And I felt it move into place. And then, from that place. . . . I felt it could have been a surge of electricity but not a shock. Again, 'liquid,' not sharp. I don't want you to think a bolt of lighting. It wasn't like that. It was soft, but it was that strong, that pronounced, from that place inside my foot out the side of my ankle. And I was almost tempted to look down to see if there had been a spark! But then, I thought, 'I don't want to move, I don't want to spoil what I'm feeling.'"

She chuckles at the recollection.

"People were still praying, yes, different people were praying aloud, and had been. A man. Then a woman. I think everybody there prayed."

Becky describes it as a "miracle experience," saying, "I could feel strength flowing. . . . I felt individually who they were . . . and that was just unreal, the whole thing was just a life-changing experience for me, because I believe in the power of healing through prayer."

After group prayer her foot felt fine. A little tender, says Becky, but it needed no medical treatment. She proceeded out of the church without assistance, bag and music in tow. "It was healed," she states. But the body was not all that was restored.

Visitation from Above

More than physical healing had occurred at the piano bench. A week later, Becky revealed the full account: While God was healing her foot, he allowed her to sense her mother's participation there in the group.

After Becky's mother died in 2001, she had begged God for a felt presence that her mother was there. "I had laid in bed, in my chair, and cried wanting Mother. 'Just come and let me see you, just come and let me talk to you, just come and let me know that you hear me.'

"I continued to pray for something, something. I did not want to necessarily see her standing at the foot of the bed or anything like that. I wanted something tangible. So that had been in my mind—and was continually in my mind—through all of this other experience I was having. . . .

"Now, back to the night I was healed. People were still praying, and I felt somebody's hand on my left shoulder, which was the shoulder next to the piano where nobody could reach. . . . I knew nobody had moved their hands. I had felt where these other hands were, and I knew nobody else could get behind me.

And so, instead of leaning over to look at her foot, she turned toward her left shoulder to see whose hand was there.

"And as I turned—I was this close—I smelled my mother. Mother didn't wear perfume. Mother didn't wear cologne very often. Every now and again Mother wore this lavender-scented toilet water. And she would wear it to church and she would wear it if they were going out to Sunday school dinners or something like that. She wore it very seldom. Mother said somebody who worked in a sewing room had no need of perfume. And she worked there [at a 'sewing hall' at Carolina Manufacturing, making men's handkerchiefs] for many years to help put all of us through school.

"When I turned around and smelled my mother, something in my heart or my soul moved the way my ankle had moved. And there was a little 'cup' that got filled up. I knew that that

16

was the tangible sign I had been asking for. . . . When I looked, of course, there was no hand on my shoulder, but I still felt it there. And as soon as I turned my head away, I didn't smell Mom anymore, but I still felt her hand on my shoulder."

She describes it not as angel wings, but as a soft, sweeping touch.

"It was not a brush . . . it was as real as if you had put your hand on my shoulder. Because what else would I have turned that way for? I wondered who could have gotten over there, that's why I turned my head. It was definitely, it was not a pressure, but it was just like you'd laid your hand on my shoulder. It was almost as tangible a filling up of that 'cup' as the thing was that filled up the little place in my foot. So then the prayer ended and people were leaving."

Becky says that although she desperately needed extra prayer that night, she probably would not have sought it. She's a natural "hugger" who loves people. And yet, she resists asking for assistance and tends to go it alone.

"As I say, I have been divorced longer than most people have been alive. So, of natural inclination or of necessity, I'm an independent cuss. I take after my mother in that respect, too. And it's very hard, it always has been, and probably—Lord help me—always will be for me to ask for help for anything. I probably would not have asked for prayer that night. . . .

"Well, I received all this other, this blessing, this miracle. And I feel that I received the rest of my life from it. Because I don't think I could have continued on very much longer without that manifestation. I was really heartsick."

Homeplace Goes Up in Flames

Another test came eight months later, when her mother's old house in Travelers Rest where they all grew up burned to the ground. The family rescued some of the most cherished furniture, photos, and the Bible that Becky had given her mother, margin notes and all. But despite that loss, "I've not had that debilitating grief, this bereft abandonment. Not only do I know

17

Mother was there [in the church], but God was there!" she says. She and her sister's family rebuilt a house on the same property, in sight of the hills. Other relatives live on adjacent land.

One Last Change, Forever

Becky cites yet another transformation—in her estimation of people. She has reassessed the character of people in need, like those of all walks of life who often come to Triune for help. Her former volunteer attitude, though well-intended, was "wrongheaded." Now she knows that the people she comes to help often bless her far, far more.

"The people themselves, their prayers, their lives, their worries, their pains, their trials, their temptations, their tears, their laughter, are my tears, my laughter. It connects me to life in a way that nothing else ever has. So I feel more alive than I've ever felt. . . . When I walk into Triune sanctuary, I can feel the breath of God. I can almost hear it, especially if you get there early and there's no one talking to each other."

The week after her fall, Becky attended choir practice as usual. She confided the full account to the same formerly homeless woman from the Salvation Army who had helped her, when injured, at the church door. Listening carefully, this new friend (who struggles with health problems and a disabled arm) understood and celebrated. Hadn't she herself just landed a solid job? A true victory? "Ain't that just like God? He healed your foot and your heart at the same time!"

Becky observes, "When she said that, I almost fell apart. Not only for what she said, but because so many people discount what people like her say, and think that they have nothing of value to say to us. And that is one of the most profound statements of theology I have ever heard . . . it's a continuation of the miracle. When I tell you that story, I have to tell that part of it."

Author's note: Becky has suffered health problems as of late, but hopes to return.

5

The Clinton Cop Who Trusted Miracles

As a couple, Edna Ellison was always more analytical and her policeman husband, though practical, was the highly intuitive one. Thinking back several decades, Edna now believes their partnership broke the stereotypical mold. For instance, what the officer dreamed at night often materialized during the day. The divine leadings he sensed and followed frequently steered him though tense moments in the line of duty.

Jesse Theodore Ellison came by his nickname "Snow" early on because he had white hair as a boy. Years later, while serving on the streets of his hometown of Clinton, South Carolina, Officer Ellison learned to place confidence in God's unseen hand. He "began to trust the miracles" just as other people depend only on straight, hard facts. In hindsight, his widow Edna reflects, "One thing I know about Snow from being married to him is he often had dreams that related to the next day's real world—and they came true."

For instance, one night before joining the police force, Snow was called in to work at another job at 2:20 a.m. When the telephone rang, it interrupted a dream he was having about driving a car, turning a curve in the road, and then running into a herd of white elephants. He dressed quickly and headed out with that vision still in mind. Driving toward town, as Snow rounded a bend in the road, he realized that it was exactly like the one in his dream. So, responding to instinct in the wee morning hours, he put on his brakes.

"And someone's white Brahman cows—four or five—were standing in the road and he was able to avoid them because he had put on the brakes," says Edna. "He thanked God for forewarning him in the dream. He had already hit the brakes in anticipation of trouble."

Another time, years later in 1975, Snow was standing on a corner looking at a nearby railroad crossing and saw a train going by. It was quite long. As he watched, a husband and wife pulled up to the intersection in their car and waited, clearly ready to drive across the tracks as soon as the train passed. There were three sets of tracks side by side, and much to his horror, Snow could see another train quickly approaching from the opposite direction. The officer could see all this from where he was standing, but the passengers could not.

"There were several sets of railroad tracks. The couple had driven across the first track, but were waiting for the train on No. 2 track to clear the second set of tracks as the next train bore down on them from the opposite direction on the third track! The train on track No. 2 obstructed their view," explains Edna.

Snow would have to dash for the car to avert disaster.

Now the officer was muscular and fit, but not fast, explains Edna. More prone to backyard badminton and roller skating than road races. "He could not run more than a few feet! He was a forty-three-year-old man who hadn't run sprints in years," Edna says, laughing. "And my husband suddenly realized that the train would clear but there would be another train *right on top of them* if they drove onto the tracks. And he began to run and he realized halfway that there was no way for him to make it before they were smashed by the oncoming train just out of sight.

"And suddenly he felt something just like *a push from behind* and he began to run faster than he was capable of running." The car was crawling forward by then. But Snow made it in time to scream and flail his hands in the air and they saw him and stopped *just* as the oncoming train missed their car

20

by inches. "He relaxed then and thanked God for whatever miraculous power enabled him to run faster than possible. He was holding his knees as he bent down to catch his breath," says Edna.

That day, the couple simply smiled and nodded at the frantic policeman's warning and drove on across the tracks after the second train had passed, blithely unaware of their brush with death until several months later. That's when Snow saw them in town and explained the close call.

"Snow did have a chance to talk with them, and it seemed they never even realized what a miracle it had been that he was in a position to see the train from afar. Somehow they had not realized how dangerous a spot they had been in," Edna says. "They did thank him over and over, once they understood the sequence of events. They knew he had saved their lives and were thankful God had allowed him to see the danger in time."

Snow believed that Divine strength—not mere adrenaline— had enabled him to reach the car in time. "Yes, he did consider this a true miracle. He felt God expanded him several times . . . to be larger than life. It was as if a miracle was taking place right before his eyes," says Edna.

On numerous occasions, small-town law enforcement allowed Snow to be involved in events beyond this everyday world, she adds. Once, the officer was called to a domestic disturbance at a house. The distraught wife burst onto the porch in a thin shift. She was shivering with panic in the cold night air. Her husband had a shotgun pointed to his neck, she said. He was threatening the entire family. She begged Officer Ellison to come in, and he did so without hesitation.

When Snow entered, the husband was positioned on a sofa, half-hidden by the door. He was a mountain logger, "a giant man," the largest man Snow had ever seen. One of his arms was as big around as Snow's thigh. And there he sat on the couch with his toe on the trigger and the muzzle of the shotgun under his chin.

21

Edna recalls Snow's thoughts. He later shared with her that he believed if he had rushed the man, the logger would have blown his head off and this would have been Snow's fault. If Snow had shot him, the man might have turned his gun on the wife and family. So another course of action presented itself—out of the blue.

"And my husband felt words coming out of him, words that were not his. In fact, the vocabulary was not his. He began to speak in the tenderest, sweetest tone to that man: 'You don't need to lose hope for the future. There's a good future waiting for you. Your wife and children love you. You have colleagues and friends that love you.' Snow said later that he didn't know if the words were true or not. And he did not ordinarily use words like 'colleague.'"

The man moved a toe. Momentarily his foot relaxed.

"And at that point my husband just moved over very strongly and took the gun. He later said, 'I believed God was using me in some miracle way—and I didn't understand it.'"

Further considering the past, Edna remembers Snow's dream one night about a car with a fountain of water spewing out the top. An almost comical image, it was. The next day, Snow (who grew up working on cars) opened the hood of his aunt's automobile and found "a perfect fountain of oil and gas" flowing up from the carburetor. Because of the previous night's dream, he was unperturbed, saying, "This is something I can do because God called me to do it."

And yet another precognition came true, as they so often did. It was a glorious spring day of spiritual encounters in the sleepy Clinton countryside. When Snow set out with his tractor to plow a garden plot down the road, he tossed back these words at his wife, "I have prayed that God will give me a lot of people to witness to today!" As he rode away in a spurt of dust, Edna mused that he'd not likely see a soul while working the solitary land.

But Snow was right. The lifelong Baptist first saw a timber company representative, who asked if his firm could buy the nearby pine forest for pulpwood. He stayed and learned about a more important subject—Jesus. Snow then saw a hunter emerge from the pines. They got to talking and Snow soon discussed Christ with him as well. Still another man along the country road was lost and stopped to ask directions. "And I wonder that you didn't come here because you are spiritually lost," confided Snow to the stranger. And finally, when the thirsty plowman sought out a country store for a drink to put with his peanut butter sandwich, he found a way to discuss spiritual matters there as well—thereby fulfilling his early morning prayer and parting prediction to Edna.

Years passed and Snow moved over to the Clinton Fire Department. In one of his worst assignments, six children and their mother had all burned to death in the attic loft of a little country house. No one nearby saw the blaze until the home was totally consumed. The chimney fell, and the ashes measured up to four feet deep. As the father stood nearby weeping, the task fell to Snow to find the bodies. A devastating fire scene often means several grisly days of searching, "And of course, he felt totally inadequate," says Edna.

But without warning, Snow heard a soft voice inside his head. Edna recalls his words: "God whispered in my ear, 'Look over here.' And I turned a stream of water in that direction and found a body. Then, 'Look over here'—another one. Another audible voice directed. . . .'" And in a matter of a few minutes, Snow had located all those children's bodies. The mother was discovered, too. "Sometimes it takes days for firefighters to find bodies, especially children's. He knew the family was grieving and wanted to account for everyone," explains Edna.

Snow himself followed suit not long after, dying in 1980 at age forty-eight. He left a wife, son, and daughter. Even so, Divine contacts continued, as "he 'spoke' to people at the funeral," says Edna. During the service, several of Snow's friends felt literal taps on the shoulder that changed their lives forever.

One notable case was a pallbearer. As young marrieds, he and his wife had lost their first child in a tragic accident while at play. The Ellisons befriended them, but grief engulfed the couple and the sorrowful husband drifted from God. Years passed. But after Snow's funeral, the husband admitted to Edna, "Before, I did not want to go to heaven, but at the funeral I heard Snow whisper in my ear, 'I've already made it right with your son. You can come on home.'" Today that man is active in his church and community, says Edna.

Others, too, came forth and told of funeral messages from Snow. But this only confirmed what Edna already knew: "There's another side—and he's alive."

Author's note: Edna Ellison, Ph.D., experiences Divine intervention in daily life. She speaks at Christian retreats and conferences in the United States and abroad. The Spartanburg resident has written sixteen books and recently taught English at North Greenville University. She has two children and one granddaughter.

6

Invisible Shield of Protection

Roland Delateja says he was doing simple yard work and chores around the house in Greenville when the inexplicable happened. Even now, the man's eyes grow wide and expressive at what transpired in August of 2006.

"There's no logical explanation," says Roland, puzzled but grinning at the recollection.

That day the recent New Jersey transplant in his early thirties was braving the South Carolina heat when he momentarily stopped yard work to grab something out of the garage. Roland, in search of a cleaning product, pulled a container of muriatic acid out of a thick rubber storage bin. He had no idea that the chemical had leached through the plastic and a hole was dripping acid.

"Upon picking up the jug of muriatic acid, it spilled down my leg and on my hands," Roland recalls with horror. "And I had on some type of nylon shorts and they have actual slits, you can actually see where the chemical penetrated through the fabric and there are holes in the shorts. So naturally, I ran inside and tried rinsing, washing myself off."

Despite every promise of injury, Roland maintains that there were no acid burns at all, no marks on his skin whatsoever. Strange indeed. The man was amazed.

"And I realized that I had just experienced a miracle, because there would be no way that I could—in that amount of time—address getting the chemical off my body, because muriatic acid is a very strong acid . . . it got on my hands, into my fingers. And I didn't think about it until after the fact that there would be no way that I could wash this chemical off my hands without it burning through. It goes through . . . layers of skin.

"So God protected me, immediately. Nothing happened to my leg or my hands. And when I had lifted the jar out of the container, it burned a hole in the garage, like a little hole [on the floor]. So nobody can explain, there's no other way to explain it! That was a miracle. God protected me from having a third-degree burn or however a doctor would categorize it, from having severe burns. I believe that I was healed instantly, that's the only way I can [explain it]. . . . It's like it never happened. But yet I have proof. The shorts—I saved them as a testimony to show how much we take for granted. I guess that as a believer I believe that He protects us. Oh, I believe His protection was over me. There's no other way to explain it."

Since this miracle, Roland has returned to his native New Jersey, where he once studied business in college and may finish his degree. Academic work explained the rigors of business, the 1-2-3s of math. But his long-held Roman Catholic faith expressed the mysteries of the unseen.

"It happened instantly. It bore a hole in my garage floor. Why wouldn't it penetrate my skin and my leg? I realized—it didn't take me hours to figure out—I mean, I know that I have had a lot of miracles in my life that I've taken for granted or never thought about, but just such a simple thing like that— science can't explain it."

7

A Visit with Jesus

A lifetime of Roman Catholicism prepared Gerrie Paschall for the fact that spiritual encounters do exist. Plus, her Italian mother back in New Jersey had prayed constantly and lived a compassionate life in touch with the Divine. Crosses and other sacred objects were in practically every room of the house, recalls Gerrie. But nothing equipped this straight-talking, information technology expert for the waking vision she had with Jesus—walking as a child with Him alongside her in Jerusalem.

Gerrie experienced what she describes as a visitation from the Lord between the hours of noon and 1 p.m. in June 2006. At the time she was a fairly new arrival to South Carolina, along with son Roland (see the previous chapter). Her mystical experience coincided with City Prayer, which the two often attended. The vision also occurred at a time in life when her spirit was growing new roots.

"When they were praying, I was praying at home. And I guess it was shortly after I had started reading the Bible and being constantly attacked by the devil. So at the time, I knelt down beside my bed and I was praying for Him to protect me against the devil."

While giving account of that day, Gerrie pauses to interject some personal history.

"He [Jesus] had come to me in my younger years when I'd been troubled with something . . . I could feel His hand. He'd usually approach me from the back and put His hand on my shoulder to let me know He was there.

"That's not the way it happened this time. He actually appeared to me larger than life, and I was fully awake, as if a curtain were opening in a Broadway play. And there He was, on a rock in Jerusalem. I knew it was Jerusalem. A tremendous rock. I did not see Jerusalem, but spiritually I knew that it was. And He sat there, very unassuming, and I was a child. In my dream I was a child, and I'm sixty years old right now. He held me in His arms, He kissed me on the side of my face and on my forehead, and He knew I was afraid. So He was almost holding me like a grandmother would hold you, knowing your fear.

"He knew everything about me. We did not verbally communicate. I call it mental but it was spiritual, heart-to-heart. He knew me and I knew him. There was nothing foreign to me about Him or vice versa. I was very comfortable with Him. I know that He did not speak my language. I knew that. So I did not even hear His voice. There was no need to speak verbally.

"He was very large of stature, a large face. He had long hair. He had no odor. There was no odor about Him, because I'm into senses. When He kissed me, you know you can usually get a person's [scent]? There was no scent at all. No breath, no hair odor. As we were sitting there very comfortably, He had me in His arms, the devil appeared—grotesque, almost giant-like. Had grotesque wings, grotesque face."

At this crisis point, it was hard for Gerrie to differentiate whose presence she was in. Was it Jesus or was it the devil? "Perhaps it was both" at the same time, she surmises. All the while, her eyes remained wide open and she could still see her bedroom.

And then suddenly, still cradling the "little girl Gerrie" protectively, the Lord "just very gently nudged the devil over this large rock. I felt no movement in His upper body. There was no anger when He did it. He put him back in his place and I knew that the devil was being driven into hell. This was all heart-to-heart. He sent him back. There was no discussion. But His body didn't tense up. There was nothing imminently hateful. It was almost like putting somebody in their proper place.

28

"It didn't end there. He kept holding me and then we started to walk and we walked for such a long time. And I said to Him, spiritually, 'Don't you have anything better to do than to spend all this time with me?' It was astounding that God would spend that kind of time with me."

Gerrie describes the scene as very "childlike." The two walked over rocks, viewing Jerusalem together. Jesus, she notes, had a much more mature face than is commonly depicted in art.

"And He kind of just looked at me—He didn't smile—as if to say, 'This is why I'm here.' It was the most comfortable feeling. It wasn't 'God/human.' We were all on the same plane. But He was as familiar as, my best analogy is, as familiar as a grandmother. Not even a mother. As a grandmother is with a grandchild. That's that comfort zone I had with Him."

And abruptly, He disappeared. That was it. Gerrie grabbed pen and paper and wrote it all down as quickly as possible.

Although she has never traveled to the Holy Land, Gerrie has no doubt that the whole scene unfolded there. "Yes, I mean, I don't just talk wildly. I knew it was Jerusalem. I was lucid, awake, in my bedroom, no drugs, no alcohol."

Surprisingly, even now Gerrie does not dig up layered meanings of this dream-vision. She just accepts it. Given time's passage, she cannot decipher more. It was a blessing, unasked for but appreciated. "All I knew is I had the peace of God on me, the protection. But I didn't go beyond that. My interpretation is extremely simple."

And yet she revisits it in her imagination, saying, "Yes. I go back to that comfort, that protection, under His protection. And I try to mirror it, knowing . . . the devil hasn't attacked me in a long, long time. I know that he's in his place, kind of put him in his place. I feel very protected. I can't go beyond that interpretation."

Gerrie says her conversations about the Lord may sound casual. But if so, it's only because through a life lived, she understands God's presence.

"I have felt him before in this same way. To me, God or Jesus is somebody that could be sitting next to me. He's not 'larger than life' to me, meaning 'threatening.' He's in my realm—I say that respectfully. I'm not elevating myself. I'm saying that He's in me. There's no question about it. He's in all of us. That's that bond I really have with Him. And I've had it as a young child, never knowing what it was. That's my gift in life."

Gerrie explains her supernatural story while sitting in a clattering, chattering Greenville favorite: Tommy's Country Ham House, which serves up southern fried chicken, corn bread, and fresh vegetables. Her plate empty and sweet tea replenished, she produces the papers she scribbled that day as "proof" of the spiritual realm. It is now summer 2007.

"I wrote down, these words are coming from Him: 'Jesus is selfless. He is all love. He loves us with a love we have not experienced on earth. He said we're precious to Him as a grandmother feels about her grandchild. He's very comfortable. I knew that I was His child. He knew everything that I was about, personally, my needs. He's patient. He does not have an agenda. He personalizes His communication to us. It is obvious to me that He is the creator, that He created me.'

"You know I don't talk like this!" she says, laughing and laying the sheets aside on the table. "That's why I wrote it down. Like, 'Who's writing this?'"

Who, indeed?

Author's note: Gerrie has returned to New Jersey and works in New York City.

8

Angel Encampment
Man Greets Unseen Servants

Doug Parrott, a newspaper field rep in the Upstate, has encountered angels at least three times. The first was while growing up in Michigan.

Playground Protection

Perhaps most children are born believers. Maybe most accept supernatural events without elaboration, as Doug did in this story. For youngsters, a nudge by an invisible angel messenger is usually perceived as a blessing, not a problem to work through or reason out (although mature reflection later can bring wisdom).

Along those lines, one of Doug's liveliest boyhood memories is being cared for by an angel.

"As a child, I did attend Angel Elementary School in Muskegon, Michigan. I was not a little angel. The principal definitely believed in corporal punishment, especially for those that would throw snowballs at safety patrols," recalls Doug.

One average day, he was running around making noise and having fun with his friends on the playground swing set.

"It had an A-frame on the end with a connecting bar. Well, I was sitting on this bar. I must have been five or six years old, maybe. And I remember falling off this bar backwards, heading to the ground.

"And literally, a hand came up and lowered me to the ground! I was caught in somebody's hand and lowered down very slowly. It was like time-stop. There was nobody there [no adult to do this]. And everybody was sitting there looking at me, as if to say, 'Are you okay?' There was nothing, I mean absolutely nothing, wrong with me—I didn't lose my breath, not bruised, not anything."

Right after the fall, Doug jumped back up good-naturedly and automatically resumed playing. At the time, he didn't process the event as anything profound.

But now at midlife and as a mature intercessor for his church and city, Doug digs deeper. He knows a heavenly being really did shield him from harm. Doug is absolutely certain he was cushioned by an unseen hand. He felt a protective palm long ago by a swing set and—even now as a grandfather—he relives that firm angel touch.

Doug says, "If you think back in your life, there are probably times when weird stuff would happen and you had no explanation for it and it just bounced off of you, especially when you were a kid."

Psalm 91 proclaims, "For he shall give his angels charge over thee, to keep thee in all thy ways."

A Guardian Speaks Audibly

Once, years ago, when Doug was still living in Michigan, a friend came up to him and said she knew how to discover the name of your own guardian angel: "You ask God to reveal the name of your guardian angel before you go to bed at night, and the first name that comes to mind in the morning is that name," she said. Her angel's name was Ferdinand.

Doug chuckled to himself. He had never heard of such a thing. He had never even considered such information. Plus, he knew there exists no pat "formula" where Divine revelation is concerned. The thought of guardian angels was interesting indeed, since the Bible does speak of "ministering angels."

That conversation occurred on a Saturday, and by Wednesday morning Doug was at his usual prayer service at a United Methodist church. While there a thought came to mind.

"I decided I would ask God to reveal the name of my guardian angel," he admits. "And I was going to be very patient and wait until He told me what it was. And I had fifteen minutes. So I sat very quietly, very patiently—as patient as I can be—for fifteen minutes and nothing happened. And I thought, 'Well, it ain't going to happen this way.'"

Doug pretty much forgot the whole thing and went on with business as usual.

The following Saturday, he ate leftover chicken and rice casserole out of the refrigerator, rather lots of it. And pretty soon he started feeling ill. Eventually Doug shuffled back to the bedroom to lie down. He pulled the covers over his head in a pitiful sort of way, got much worse, and strongly felt like he was going to be sick. He got up and was about to head to the bathroom.

"I flipped the blankets off, I put my feet on the floor, and I heard the most *incredible* baritone voice say, 'David!' I cannot even describe it. It was very low, very resonant. And I turned around and said, 'No, my name is Doug.' And that's all I heard. And instantly my stomach went flat. I didn't feel like I was going to throw up anymore. I just took a nap. Sometime later that evening I was walking downtown and all of a sudden it just dawned on me that maybe my angel's name was David."

Puzzled, Doug ran the story past someone he trusted—who promptly said he was "nuts." Not being in complete agreement, he further consulted a United Methodist minister friend who, after hearing the whole story, said, "Well, it works for me!"

Eager for a second reaffirming opinion and not wishing to be rash in his assessment of such matters, Doug asked a Catholic priest and friend over for dinner and a relaxing discussion afterward. The priest's immediate response to the guardian angel story? "Well, it works for me!" And, of course, those were the precise words the Methodist pastor had said, and in the same emphatic way.

So Doug cast his private vote on this revelatory message: "From that point on *it worked for me, too,* and the name is 'David.' You know the idea of angels, they really are out there."

Commanding Image Stands at Attention

Later, in 2007, Doug physically viewed an immense angel. This occurred in Florida at a healing weekend at an Episcopal church. During one session, a priest stood in the middle of the chapel, in the aisle between the pews, and laid his hands on people in prayer. Various other lay prayer ministers did likewise. "There was a lot of activity in the room," says Doug, who was quietly down on his knees at the time.

Suddenly, Doug raised his head from prayer and saw something out of the ordinary. "And I just looked up and there was a 'hole' where nothing was showing up [behind the priest]. I didn't see any faces or anything, but it was huge. It was the shape of a person. It looked like a person, anyway, about nine feet high, maybe four feet across in the shoulders. It wasn't a solid being. But light from behind it wasn't coming through. I didn't see features. It was like a hole in the air where this was."

Transcendent images are hard to capture in human terms, but Doug gives it a shot. Yes, the warrior presence had shape. It had substance. But there was no solidity as is commonly perceived in the daily world.

Down went Doug's head for a moment. Then he peeked at the front of the sanctuary to make sure he really saw something. "And it was still there! I didn't know what to do about it or anything. I didn't say anything to anybody at the time."

Reverently, Doug lowered his head to pray. When he lifted his eyes one last time, the figure had vanished from sight.

"It was just very strange. I wasn't frightened at all by it. In fact, I was a little bit surprised. You can imagine. You blink your eyes and you're not sure what you're seeing here. You close your eyes and open them again and it's still there. I just didn't know what to make of it. I wasn't alarmed. In fact, I was actually kind of comforted! I said, 'This is a good place to be.' I honestly believe that this angel was sent for protection. It was an angel of protection for this priest because the work that he was doing wasn't making Satan real happy. And I honestly believe that this angel was sent to protect everyone in this sanctuary at this particular time."

From personal experience, research, and deep consideration, Doug has decided that sentimentalized "modern" angels are inaccurate.

"Most of the time, when people see angels, they're kind of terrified—because they are big."

And apparently, close at hand.

Author's note: Doug and his wife, Cindy, who works in Spartanburg, intercede daily for their local Episcopal congregation and community. They are also linked with prayer groups for the nation and world.

9

Keys to the Kingdom

Sometimes tiny miracles shine brightest. Brenda Preston thinks so. When she recalls her ministry trip to China—one of fifty countries she has visited in the past fourteen years of teaching and speaking—Brenda is truly glad that she lost her luggage key in a town somewhere between southern China and Beijing. Because that day, she found out God even cares about such things as suitcases.

It was the early 1990s. Brenda and her husband, Tom, from Greenville were traveling with a group of thirteen to help develop Chinese business leaders. The purpose of this joint venture was to teach about business with an emphasis on ethics and "to look for opportunities to build relationships with people to share the gospel," she explains. The Prestons are affiliated with Campus Crusade for Christ International.

As the group left southern China and moved northward to Changsha, everyone was instructed to fasten suitcases carefully and keep them secured. Brenda did as she was told. But amid the confusion of travel, she misplaced her key and couldn't find it anywhere. Suddenly, here was a worrisome detail in a strange land. She had been trying so hard to follow security rules and, at the same time, pay attention to the real reason for their journey—witnessing for Christ. She searched her purse and pockets as they boarded a van heading north toward Beijing. Still, no key.

The travelers consisted of mixed couples and singles. So no one would stay alone, Brenda was assigned Lynn Mitchell of

Greenville as roommate for the duration, while Tom roomed with a man from the ministry group. Brenda and Lynn sat together during the five-hour van ride, "and the whole time my friend and I, we're praying, 'What are we going to do, we've lost the key?' And I'm thinking, 'How am I going to get in my suitcase when I get there?'"

When the travelers arrived for the night, Brenda found that their prayers had gone before them. A surprise was waiting at their hotel. Brenda remembers exactly how it happened.

"Lynn and I go up to our room and we open the door and we look down and there's a key on the floor. And it's just a little, tiny key. And so we go in and I pick this little key up and think, 'Oh, my goodness, this is a key to a suitcase.' And then I go and put it in the lock to my suitcase and it unlocks it. And Lynn and I just start to cry and thank God because we know this was a miracle. God had done that.

"And not only did we see Him there, but it prepared us for the rest of the trip in anticipation for what God was going to do."

Sure enough, the entire eighteen days in China were loaded with celestial events, says Brenda, including what she labeled "the biggest miracle"—when three women in the city of Dalian listened carefully to the gospel as she explained it, and then accepted Christ as savior.

Yes, on one level that key was generic, ordinary, one common to perhaps many suitcases around the world. But Brenda points out that, on another level, the prayer-answered provision of a seemingly trivial suitcase key symbolized efforts to unlock the entire nation of China to the spread of Christianity. This land was closed to all missionary inroads for many years, and often is today, at least publicly.

"Finding that key and His doing that was just a way of showing how much He loves and how much He cares about even the small things," she explains. "Lynn and I, our lives have never been the same since then. Because when we see each other and we are praying about something that looks absolutely impossible, we just look at each other and say, 'The Key.' And then we think, 'God, you can do anything. If you can do that. . . .' And that cannot be a coincidence, to me. That little key was there. We just opened the door and it's lying right there on the floor."

10

Voice Saves Publisher and Son

When the publisher of this book called to suggest the project, he shared a curious tale of his own. In July of 2004, a Voice had stopped him from colliding with a speeding tractor-trailer— thereby sparing Derik Shelor and his son, Jonathan, age three at the time.

This unusual event interjected both comforts and troubles into Derik to this day. The "whys," the "ifs."

Derik grew up in Charleston. Several years ago he and his wife were living in Erin's hometown of Greenville while she taught in the Furman University history department and he worked as a freelance copy editor. On the summer day that could have changed—or erased—their lives, Derik and Jonathan were driving down Roe Ford Road toward the Berea Branch Library. An average trip, they thought.

Derik confides that he and his wife of fifteen years rarely argue. But one of his pet peeves, admittedly, is this: Erin tells him the light is green the moment it changes, implying that he needs to go, while he tends to want to wait a brief moment, just in case someone runs the light. It's petty, he says, but there it is.

On this particular day, Derik was feeling "a little grumpy" for reasons he now cannot recall. The mood wasn't typical, and perhaps his reaction to it made him a bit careless. When the car reached a red light at the intersection of Roe Ford and White Horse Road, he thought with mild irritation, "Well, as soon as it turns green I'm just going to gun it and go.

"And then I heard a Voice that said, 'Wait.' It wasn't a commanding voice. It wasn't a thundering voice. It just said, 'Wait.' A male voice, middle-aged. I don't know if it was my conscious, or my subconscious, or God or Jesus, or maybe my grandfather trying to save his great-grandson. But I waited a second, and an eighteen-wheeler came plowing through the intersection. I remember watching the gray trailer fly by, sitting there for a moment, then looking all around the car to see where the Voice had come from."

Today, Derik, Erin, Jonathan (now seven), and two-year-old Elizabeth are happily settled in Pennsylvania. But Derik has never forgotten that defining moment at a South Carolina intersection. Questions arise in his mind, especially since so many people die daily in traffic accidents and other split-second mishaps. Why, in a word, were he and his son saved?

He is not sure. But two things stand out: One, this was not imagined. An actual, authentic Voice spoke directly to him. And two, they would have been killed in an instant—or all-but-killed—if he had not hesitated one second at Someone's request.

"And as for why, honestly, part of me says perhaps it wasn't about me at all." The event raises a number of possibilities in Derik's mind. Maybe Whoever spoke did so "to save Jonathan's grandson fifty years down the road," he says. "Or maybe it happened to keep the EMS worker from losing faith when Jonathan died in her arms. . . ."

Another possibility, he says: Perhaps it happened to save the truck driver. Or even the *contents* of the truck. Or maybe the accident-in-progress was stopped to save another driver in the oncoming lane.

Practically speaking, Derik says, "It's a lot easier to stop a car that's sitting still than it is to stop a big truck like that."

Or the answer could combine all of the above and many other unknown factors, plus one more. "Maybe it happened so that I would see that this book gets written and published," Derik says, adding, "The regrettable thing about all this is that it wasn't a drop-to-my-knees sort of experience for me. I wish it had been. I'm not a Christian yet. Maybe someday. But it was real."

Author's note: I find Derik's story not only credible, but somewhat familiar and totally in line with other miracles I have heard. One day in 1995 or thereabout, I myself heard a Voice that possibly saved me from entanglement in a horrific wreck on South Pleasantburg Drive in Greenville. In my case, the Messenger spoke in gentlemanly fashion as I waited first in line at a large intersection, saying, "It would be better if you turned left," instead of going straight as planned. I obeyed, heeding the interior warning but not wanting to do so. I didn't want to change directions. The whole thing operated against common sense and I felt silly—even though alone in the car— yet I was compelled to turn left. I drove somewhere or other and don't recall where. But minutes later, when retracing my path through the same intersection, "straight ahead" was packed with more ambulances and fire trucks than I had ever seen. Yes, the Voice was real.

11

Mama's Parting Phone Call

Lib Burlington is as down-to-earth as the rich soil in Travelers Rest where she and husband Dave plant their vegetables and fuss over their blooms and bushes. And yet, this adventurous baby boomer has seen plenty of excitement. Her career has arched from Lowcountry radio disk jockey to project controls employee at Fluor to (most recently) front desk librarian at the Berea Branch Library. Quite a stretch, with interesting little stops in between. But nothing has topped the two supernatural messages she received from heaven after her mother passed away.

Lib experienced both within one year of her mother's death. Florence "Flo" Elizabeth Arant of Orangeburg died on August 4, 2001, pre-deceased by husband Harry, a local oral surgeon. They left behind three grown daughters and a firstborn son. Now in his mid-fifties and living in Orangeburg, Harry Basil Arant III has severe Down syndrome, Alzheimer's, and Parkinson's disease. He lives in a group home.

"My mother never thought, and neither did we, that Basil would outlive them—but he did. And she always worried what would happen if she died and he was still there. What would happen to him."

Miracles, "you either believe them or you don't," muses Lib, "but it happened to me. There's nothing unique about me. I'm grounded in reality. It just happened."

Up to this point, Lib has been somewhat protective of her story. She has carefully selected just who she would tell it to and when, ever mindful to stick to the facts and never titillate with dramatic details just for effect. Now she believes that sharing a true intervention by God does people much spiritual good, somewhat like fortifying the soul with a balanced meal.

"It anchors them. They go, 'Whoa'—it's almost like they wish something like that would happen to them! And I wish for them, that it had happened to them, too. But my circumstances were unique, in that Basil is my brother."

Heaven Touches Earth

The first surprising event happened in February 2002, about six months after Flo's death.

In Lib's words: "Basil calls me at least five or six times a day. So he called me one day and there was nothing unusual about this phone call, nothing at all. We always talk about 'What did you do today? What are you going to eat for supper?' And as we were talking, all of a sudden the phone crackled like there was lightning or something. And I said, 'Basil?' because I thought we had lost the connection.

"And I heard my mother's voice. It was on the phone. It was on the phone! I was trying not to believe it because I'd never had anything like this happen before and I knew she was gone, she had passed away. So I heard her voice and I heard her say, 'Honey?' and I said, 'Basil?' because I was just trying to reconnect with him and he didn't seem to be on the phone anymore. I said again, 'Basil?' and I then heard my mother say, 'Honey . . . ,' and I repeated, 'Basil?' And she said, '*Are you going to take care of him?*' And I said, 'Basil, are you still on the phone?'

"I tried so hard just to . . . I don't know why I was trying to push it away. It was like I didn't want to believe it, but yet. . . . And then she asked me one more time, '*Are you going to take care of him?*' And I said, 'Yes ma'am, I will take care of him. I'll always take care of him." And then she said something else. I couldn't quite understand it. Then I heard Basil say, 'G!' That's what he calls me—'G' because I used to be a disc jockey and he would call me a 'G-jockey' and he shortened it to 'G,' so he's always called me 'G' for years. And I said, 'Did you just hear Mama on the telephone?'"

Though his mental faculties are greatly diminished, her brother of course feels quite deeply and understands that their mother is gone, says Lib.

"And he replied, 'No.' I said, 'Is [group home] staff in your room?' He said, 'No.' I asked, 'Did you hand the phone to someone?' He said, 'No.' And I said, 'Thank you Lord, thank you.' I knew—and I knew right then—that he was mine. That he was mine to take care of, because my husband and I never had children. I never understood why we didn't. But now I understood why and I've kept that promise. Actually, I'm now his legal guardian."

Lib says the voice on the other end of the phone was totally audible. "You never forget your mother's voice, you *never* forget your mother's voice. And it was *her*."

When Flo's question came, Lib was put to the test. It was a directive, a probing question from beyond. Yet, it never crossed Lib's mind to turn her mother down and not take full responsibility for her disabled brother, though she struggled with the fact that it was actually happening. Both of Lib's sisters have children of their own to care for, and "from the get-go" Lib and Basil have always been particularly close. The phone call simply confirmed what the next step should be.

"I wish that I could almost rewind and say, 'Let me ask you some things.' But the only thing that was necessary was for me to accept, and she to ask. And that's what it all boiled down to. I was at a crossroads and I could have gone either way. And I'm so glad I told her 'yes.' I am *so* glad. And I haven't regretted it. It's been a challenge but it has been wonderful. I have grown so much taking care of him."

The Scent of Her Presence

Lib's second brush with the hereafter occurred one year after her mother's death, almost to the day. Lib and her sister had decided to go antique shopping on Main Street in Travelers

44

Rest. They were browsing in the back room of a shop. Lib remembers the time distinctly: two o'clock in afternoon.

"I was standing at a table and all of a sudden I felt this breeze. And I knew that my mother was there. What confirmed it was I suddenly could smell her perfume. I just stood there and I went, 'Mama!' And I was just so happy, just so happy. I knew she was there. I looked down at the table and there was a little sachet pillow with a picture of a dog on it that's the type of dog from *The Wizard of Oz*—Toto. And underneath the dog was the dog's name, Buddy. Well, my mother had this dog when she was a little girl . . . and his name was Buddy. What was so sad was, they had to put this dog down when she was a little girl because he was bitten by a rabid raccoon. She loved that dog and she missed that dog. Anyway, his name was Buddy. I said, 'Oh, I need to buy this sachet pillow and I know who I'm going to send it to—our little sister Deryl.'"

So the two headed home, with Lib saying, "I'm going to mail that thing first thing Monday to Deryl."

About thirty minutes after they returned to Lib's house, the phone rang and it was Deryl. "And I said, 'Oh, I'm so glad you called. I've got something to tell you.' She said, 'Me first!' And I said, 'Okay, you first. You go ahead.' She said, 'Lib, remember when we were little? We said that if something happened and we told each other, that we would believe each other.' I said, 'Absolutely.' She told me, 'I'm going to tell you something and you're going to probably think I'm crazy, but believe me, this happened.' I said, 'I promise you. I'll believe you.'"

That very afternoon, Deryl was in her Orangeburg yard, cutting the grass on her riding lawnmower. The legendary Lowcountry heat was withering, as usual. Absolutely no wind blew. "Deryl related that she pulled up in her driveway and stopped. She turned off the tractor and all of a sudden she felt a breeze. Why, I just got chill bumps, and she said, 'Lib, then I smelled her perfume. It was Mama.' I said, 'Deryl, what time did that happen?' It was simultaneous. It was two o'clock in the afternoon. 'Lib,' Deryl said, 'I know it was her.'

"I responded, 'Oh Deryl, I've got to tell you.' Then I told her about the sachet pillow. I said, 'Deryl, you are not going to believe this. But of course you will, because it happened to me. I'm mailing you this pillow because I know that you need this.'"

Lib confirms from her sister that, no matter how impossible in the unbearable heat, "there was a breeze, and there was her perfume. It was Chanel No. 5 . . . her signature fragrance." Lib says, "It meant the world to Deryl that she got that visitation from her."

These are the only two times that Lib's mother has "spoken," but they were more than sufficient to bless her children many times over.

"I knew she was there. There's no doubt in my mind," says Lib. "My sisters and I—we cut up a lot, we love each other, but we believe in each other. And I would've believed her. What made it so unique and so special for Deryl and me was that it happened at the same time. It was the exact same type smell, the same breeze, and also there was the connection of the sachet pillow. I knew to buy it and to send it to her, not knowing at that time she had had the same breeze and perfume experience. How would I know to send it to her? It was metaphysical. And she's got that sachet pillow sitting right up on her dresser."

Coming Forward to Share

Lib grieved so hard when her mother died. But up until this interview, she's been hesitant to put words to this story. One reason: people might not believe her. Or, they might surmise, "'Maybe she's just not 'all there.' She was just grieving too hard for her mother! But I have pulled on those memories. It's just like it happened yesterday. It won't fade. Like I say, it was just a gift. I've never looked back on it with any type of remorse. I'm so glad it happened."

Furthermore, her mother's messages explain why she is now a serious "mom" herself—Basil's appointed, primary caretaker.

"I have to stay grounded. I don't have another option—now that I'm a parent, you just don't take a day off."

Lib, a Methodist, still reflects on the deeper meaning of the two beyond-the-grave encounters.

"The first visit was Mama needing to confirm with me that I would take care of Basil. . . . I needed to reassure her that we'll take care of him. But she needed to get my attention, too. She really did, and she got it. Not that I wasn't taking care of him, but I suddenly needed to go to the courts. My husband is an attorney. I mean, we even did things such as drawing up a living will. We got smart about his care."

Regarding the pillow-and-perfume moment, "It was just a gift to me, a gift to let me know that she's there, she's with me always. She's pleased with me and she likes what I'm doing."

Finally, in their own way the sachet pillow and wafting perfume validated all three sisters as truth-tellers and brought them closer together. "Deryl had an experience identical to mine, just in a different place."

Author's note: Lib Burlington grew up in Orangeburg and still has family there. This is the first time she has expressed her experience publicly. She found it particularly gratifying to be interviewed on Mother's Day 2007.

12

The Lawyer Befriended by Angels

When the late Preston Reid still strolled the streets of the Palmetto State, he was no stranger to courtroom battles. He was equally at home at tense, high-velocity Greenville High football games. Or at ease at the kitchen table alongside his wife, Susan, and their family of five boys—often with multiple friends attached. And whenever in Charleston to see any of their sons at The Citadel (four graduated and one still attends), nothing grabbed Preston's heart like the American flag presiding over a field of stoic cadets in dress whites and the sound of the bagpipes leading the cadets with "Scotland the Brave." But beyond these human scenes and many more, Preston reverenced the silent messages of angels sent from Above. He drew comfort from God and His angels. There's no way around it: From boyhood, Preston was part earthbound, part mystic.

"Since early childhood, Preston felt like there was always a 'presence' around him" that brought comfort, says Susan, who lost her husband of twenty-nine years to cancer in February 2007. He was fifty-three.

This reliance on unseen helpers probably started when Preston was very young and his little brother fell off a high porch and cracked his head open, recalls Susan. Preston felt like his brother probably wouldn't live, so he fervently prayed that he would.

"He talked to his three angels then . . . he always felt like his prayers had been answered that day and they were at his side. Many times when he saw someone really struggle, he asked the three angels to help. Many times they responded," she explains.

So, although not everybody knew it, this deep experience of spiritual reality was true of Preston even before a colon cancer diagnosis rocked his world in late 2004. Whenever the jaunty and talkative Preston pulled apart from events—or sat alone for a few minutes in his woodworking shop in the backyard of his Augusta Road home or elsewhere—perhaps his thoughts drifted above the shady oaks to a world far beyond. There, as Preston sipped his customary chilled glass of tea, God and angels were present in his life.

It is easy to imagine such contemplations. And here's why. Not long after Preston got sick, for the first time he asked angels to help him. Preston had requested many times for help from the angels for others, but never for himself. A short time later, in the middle of the night while Susan was beside him in bed asleep, he saw three large, magnificent celestial beings. "He said the angels have been here: two in the room and one outside the door. He said they were huge, so big he didn't know how they fit in the room. He described their clothes. They were real simple but unbelievably beautiful. They were magnificent, but not fancy. Colors and fabrics and things like that, things that he had never seen before.

"He didn't feel like he just dreamed it. He felt like they were really there. He said that one of them was kneeling beside the bed. He [the angel] took his fist and balled his fist up and reached inside of Preston's stomach, that then he pulled his fist out and threw it [something] away. The angels left, and that's when he woke me up. I think he felt they had pulled the cancer away or pulled something out of there that shouldn't be there."

Preston said that each angel had a name and he had always known their names, which he shared with his wife. The unusual names are regal-sounding, even noble, and somewhat distant, as if from another time and place. He told Susan and all his friends that came to visit about the angels.

Though Preston was in the bed a good deal before his demise, even a week beforehand he looked surprisingly better.

He went to his doctor's office appointment "and was walking with such spirit in his step that it almost looked like a rebound. He really had energy that day," says Susan.

All along, the vision of the three angels was highly significant. "It helped him keep his faith. It helped him stay real strong, to just stay coherent until the end," says Susan. "Our understanding was that he would be bedridden for the last month. Our miracle was that he was really with us until the end. He felt like God and the angels were always with him. Even at the end his faith was very strong.

"The day before he died, he came out to the den and somebody was there to see him, and he looked around the sofa like somebody was behind it. I said, 'What are you looking at?' And he said, 'Nothing.' Then a hospice minister came, and again Preston looked around the sofa."

Susan is convinced that he saw heavenly companions or escorts: "Later I realized they were angels about to help him on his journey."

Preston's funeral at Buncombe Street United Methodist Church was one of the largest ever held in that large, overflowing sanctuary. The standing-room-only crowd probably swelled to over a thousand. The GHS football team filed in wearing red jerseys and khaki pants to honor one of their graduates and bedrock promoters. The team entered just before the family came in, sat right behind them, and remained transfixed to the speakers throughout the service ("spellbound," described one witness). During this February 27 commemoration, a son read an entry from his father's journal. Preston had written it on that exact date in 1976 as part of a University of South Carolina independent study while living at Camp Old Indian in Cleveland, South Carolina. This rather amazing, life-changing account portrayed how the Lord visited Preston's rustic hut in the woods and dialogued with him for hours.

Not long after Preston's serious illness had become known, bright red and white "Go Preston" bumper stickers sprouted up on thousands of cars, trucks, and vans throughout Greenville and surrounding communities. After his death, they still remain around town as a vital, living testimony to this "everyman" who disliked facades and moved freely among the people—and, apparently, the angels.

His hat has been bronzed and mounted inside Sirrine Stadium, where Greenville High athletic teams play.

And the legacy lives on still. In late 2007, a community-wide bone marrow drive was held in memory of Preston, who himself donated marrow in 1998 to a sixteen-year-old girl he would never meet. Susan said it was such a gift when the Reid family later met that recipient for the first time. By then she was a lovely, thriving young woman still alive because of Preston.

Somewhere in the skies, there must be a banner: "Go Preston."

13

Shifting Gears in Columbia
A Young Man's Race with Ruin

In all probability, Wilbert Evans Jr. should have died one reckless night decades ago on the streets of Columbia, South Carolina. "As He literally saves you from death, you say, 'Okay, there is *something* I have to do!'" says Wilbert without hesitation.

Now standing behind the counter of a high-end electronics store he manages in Greenville, Wilbert mentally jumps back to his carefree college days at the University of South Carolina. It was 1979 or 1980. He was twenty and dating a girl at Columbia College, several miles from downtown. Wilbert instantly relives the few seconds that nearly stole his future.

"One night we had been out on a date and I had dropped her off and was heading back to my dorm room. And so on the way back, I got into a race with another car. It was late at night, about one or two o'clock in the morning. There was no one else on the highway. On the main street, you might say. (Once you get older, you realize that was very foolish at the time. . . .) Nobody else was on the street—just me and this other vehicle. I don't know who this person was. It was just two fast cars meeting up late at night, at the same point in time, where one tries to race the other.

"And I guess we were doing about seventy or eighty miles an hour, and at that time I was driving a '72 Firebird and it was a pretty feisty car. As we were rounding a curb—it wasn't a corner, but a curb—there was a cab sitting there in the parking lot getting ready to come out into the street. And what was odd about it was he sat there. It's not like he sat there, paused, and pulled out. He kind of sat there for five seconds, which is a long time when you're approaching at eighty, ninety miles an hour."

The two racers got closer and closer to passing alongside the cab, when suddenly the taxi pulled out into Wilbert's lane, which was the left-hand lane, or passing lane. What's more, the cab *stayed* in his lane, causing Wilbert to jerk his car violently to the side to avoid a collision.

"When I swerved, I wound up across the street in a parking lot that was a very short parking lot. . . . When the car came to rest and I got out, I looked over at the passenger's side and there was a humongous light pole sitting there that I did not hit. My car did not scratch it. But it was close enough that I couldn't open the door if I were on the passenger's side, which was a perfect kind of a miss. The pole was huge—you're probably looking at about four feet in circumference. And also, I guess about ten feet away, there was another pole. So my car was in-between these two poles."

No devastation, no death, no ruin or arrest. Nothing. Wilbert got off scot-free.

When Wilbert screeched to a stop and realized he didn't hit anything, "it was like an acknowledgment. When you go through something like that and you know that it had to be an angel that took my vehicle and safely put it where it needed to be. Oh yes, God has been good to me. He has plans for me."

Wilbert believes now that God providentially protected him. But even at age twenty, he was spiritually attuned to this larger reality. "I know that I had given my heart to Christ when I was twelve (and again when I was twenty-nine, the rededication), so I knew I had a 'covering' from being twelve years old . . . it's one of those things where you know where your miracle or salvation came from, where the help came from. And being as young as I was and away from home in school, there was, like, 'Thank you, God!' and you go on with your life. But nine years later then I rededicated my life."

On impulse, Wilbert snaps open a cell phone photo of two smiling children. The African-American businessman shakes his head with wonder that his happy family life with wife and kids and so much else might have been wiped out—even before they existed.

"When it happened, it wasn't as if I was just so far into the world that I didn't know. I *knew*. I knew exactly what was going on. I just was very thankful for that. Things like that, that happen along in your life, kind of nudge you back because you know there has to be a purpose in order for Him to save you."

14

Bolt of Lightning Protects Family

He unleashes his lightning beneath the whole heaven
and sends it to the ends of the earth.

Job 37:3, NIV

Billy Mitchell of Simpsonville credits a well-timed burst of lightning with saving his family one night in Nevada back in the early 1960s. Mitchell, then serving with the U.S. Navy, lived with wife Lil and their four children in Long Beach, California. Whenever the Mitchells traveled to see Lil's family in Salt Lake City, Utah, they had to drive. The desert leg of the vacation was especially grueling back in those days, before car air conditioning was standard, so they crossed over at night.

One July evening, the Mitchells set out from California destined for Ely, Nevada, ultimately to arrive in Utah. In the car were the couple and their four young children—a daughter and three sons.

"It was extremely hot, very dark, no lights anywhere, no moon, just an extremely dark night," recalls Billy, now in his mid-seventies. "There was no fence whatsoever, just open, desert-like ranchland. As we were going down this real long grade, a bolt of lightning came out of the sky horizontally in front of us. And directly in front of us was a large herd of cattle—black cows—standing right in the middle of the road! And there was no way that I would have been able to miss those cattle, except for that lightning coming across. It illuminated it, lit up the area and everything. We saw all the cattle standing there."

Billy jammed on the brakes to avoid a crash. The car stopped just in time.

Immediately after the flash of lightning, the sky darkened to an inky backdrop. After taking a moment to regain his composure, the father stepped on the gas, inched the car through the herd, and resumed the journey unharmed. The sky remained absolutely clear, with no rain, thunder, or lightning that evening or the rest of the week.

"We got to Ely that night. We just thought that was a miracle. God intervened and He led the way for us. I was able to see those cattle and everything. I was able to come to a complete stop and get away from them and protect our children."

Furthermore, today Bill realizes how weak car headlights were back then, certainly not strong enough to shine on black Angus cattle in time to stop his car.

Another thought is the isolation of that "no man's land," as he calls it. There were no cars coming or going that night. In an age before cell phones, how would injured survivors have called for help? Likely, they would have been stranded in that arid, desert-like terrain.

All four youngsters in the car that night grew up to lead productive lives, with the oldest of those little boys later an associate pastor in the apostolic faith. Billy went on to serve twenty-one years in the Navy, the last four working and traveling with Boat Support Unit 2 to assist Navy SEALs. Post-retirement, Billy and Lil made Simpsonville their home in 1973. They are the happy grandparents of nine and great-grandparents of four.

A later chapter tells how Billy received yet another blessing—a healing considered rare in this century or in any other.

15

The One They Call the Comforter

Betsy Brown is completing a master's degree in teaching. So she naturally turns everyday events into valuable life lessons. A teacher typically does this. She thinks this way. Practically everything can be useful to learn and to teach.

Betsy has this opinion of miracles, too. For her, supernatural situations have enormous practical application.

Betsy admits that extraordinary moments are not automatic. Heavenly visitations do not materialize in everyone's life. But they do happen from time to time. And when this occurs, these visionary insights are "milestones" rich in meaning. Anyone who has moved through a waking vision or a significant dream can draw from that deep spiritual well forever.

And yet, "You don't put your faith in miracles. You don't put your faith in seeing things. You put your faith in God. And whether you see things or don't see things, really it doesn't affect the 'destination,'" says Betsy, who moved with her husband and family from Virginia to Greenville in 1992. They have two daughters.

Betsy has experienced remarkable moments. But there can be a downside to this.

"It's easy to grow dependent on . . . wishing some miraculous thing would happen," she explains, especially when times are bad. "So for the people who have never seen anything [miraculous] like that, I would say to them, 'You're actually walking along your faith path exactly as you need to, in complete faith and trust.'"

She notes Paul's words, "For we walk by faith and not by sight" (2 Corinthians 5:7).

"Part of me thinks that people who have never seen anything end up with stronger 'faith muscles.' I mean, that might seem flip-flopped, because I've seen these things and it's helped my faith. But on the other hand, I look at my husband and people like my parents who've never *seen* anything and they are just doing exactly what they are supposed to do and their faith is so strong and tremendous."

That said, Betsy shares several revelatory experiences in her life.

A Towering Presence

One took place near suppertime in late 1997 or early 1998. Betsy recalls only that the girls were small. The younger was still a baby.

Betsy was not seeking anything unusual at the time, not thinking anything special that afternoon. She was just doing the commonplace—standing at the kitchen counter cutting up chicken for dinner. The area is a light, cheerful, open design and Betsy was positioned at an island counter facing directly into the family room. A typical young mother, she always kept an ear out for the children while they were napping or playing in another part of the house.

Betsy conveys the following recollection while pointing to the spot where it occurred: "I'm just cutting up chicken, and I look over there and right by the fireplace by the bookshelf, the ceiling disappeared. And I'm wide awake! And this male presence—not a man, but a male—really tall, appears. (The number that sticks in my head is fourteen feet tall.) All I really noticed was the lower part of the light. And there were no feet. It was robe-like but it wasn't real cloth. And it wasn't just light either; it was more substantial. And nothing was said, but my reaction was really extreme."

The kitchen utensils fell from her hands onto the food. She moved several steps from where she had been standing and instantly dropped to the floor, overwhelmed.

58

"I ended up somehow right here, absolutely on my knees with my face to the floor, sobbing with love because I love Jesus Christ so much. I am sobbing with love and relief because I love Christ so much."

It was that quick: fixing food for the family one minute, and the next—breathless and face-down before a celestial visitor.

"This was not Christ," she clarifies, but "I felt pure comfort. It was just palpable, just pure comfort through every inch of my being. And I'm just sobbing with joy and I look up and it's gone."

The imposing male presence had not said anything. "He struck me as just Timeless," she says. "Very strong and vibrant," but not bound by time or place. He had a face, but she did not focus on that.

The strong phrase that suddenly came to Betsy's mind was "'The One They Call the Comforter.' Not 'The Comforter,' not 'The Holy Spirit'—I don't know. So I still call it in my mind, 'The One They Call the Comforter.'

"And what I learned from that, what I believe I learned from that, is that Christ sends the Comforter. Crying with that kind of love, it was like I felt I was born with that kind of love, and it was just opened up somehow. I didn't even realize the depth of my love for Christ until that time."

Betsy says the presence was not Jesus, but clearly representative of the Kingdom of God. "I think honestly his point was love for Christ, and Christ's love for each individual.

"Strange thing was, I didn't really need comfort at that time. I wasn't having any crisis." Betsy found herself wondering why this had happened. But within a week she had a difficult experience to deal with. And "I hung on, knowing . . . I really honestly think part of making it through was that Christ knew who I was."

What else did she learn? "I really believe from that experience that God controls time and that God knows people and what's going to happen to them and what has happened to them and how it all fits together. That was, I guess, the first time I really truly understood down in my core that God knew me. And if he knows me, then he knows every single living thing on this planet. And that's such a comfort to me, and maybe that's what comfort is.

"I realized that every life has meaning because God knows who you are and so everything matters. And I mess up all the time, but I know that." This knowledge, she says, has carried her.

Now, when Betsy prays for others, she asks "for Jesus Christ to send this loving comfort to those people. That's the important thing—Christ."

Betsy interprets that the dynamic presence she saw is directed to provide the refuge that Christ sends. "He does not act on his own. He's sent by Christ."

Out-of-time events such as this have practical use in the routine events of life, says Betsy. Hearkening back to a Divine episode helps people when they are in trouble, tempted, or scared. It soothes them. Those things such as fear "don't have real power, because *this* is real," she says of God's peace. "When you feel that kind of comfort, it can actually change your decision-making process because you're not reacting in fear, you know. And to be honest, we react in fear many times.

"The comfort was complete understanding of Christ's love for us. To me that is the definition of comfort. Comfort wasn't, 'Oh, you don't have any problems, and you'll never have any scary things again.' It didn't take anything away, that comfort. It didn't remove any scars or problems I have. It didn't take away any of that stuff, although that can happen. But that comfort was just simply understanding at a fundamental level Christ's love."

As a result, Betsy believes she is a better listener to those who share spiritual stories. Patting the kitchen counter, she smiles and says, "This stuff is just so insignificant," compared to spiritual realities. "The point is the Kingdom of Heaven is real. Nothing else is real. So maybe that's a lesson."

Another snapshot into eternity occurred when Betsy was but a girl not yet in the fourth grade, living with her parents in Charlotte, North Carolina. Betsy was in her bedroom deep in slumber, the windows closed. "And I rolled over and there was a lady praying by my bed. She was kneeled and praying, in a prayer gesture. I felt a deep peace. I didn't see her face but she had brown hair and it was blowing in the wind and she was wearing blue. And it was like this wind was blowing. I don't know who that lady was by the bed," she says, considering the long-ago memory. "She was just kind of a young adult, but I never saw her face.

"And I looked over at her and somehow I knew she was praying for the world. She wasn't praying for me. She was praying for the world. And as a small child that was the first time I realized that God was immense. He wasn't this 'Man in Heaven.' She was praying for the world to God. I was completely at peace and completely awake. The lady praying made me understand that prayer can affect the world and we can pray for the world. And we should! And from that experience, I know that prayer to God should be a continual living thing within people. As much as you breathe, you need to just pray. It's just a constant 24/7 thing."

She says many people have never seen anything they would label as miraculous. And yet she and others have. So what's the advantage of sharing these stories?

"Because I think we've backlashed so far into believing only what can be proven or measured that, as a general rule, I think community has kind of lost sight of what's real; yet these things are happening."

Betsy shares the previous account willingly and respects others who share their own experiences, when put in spiritual context and with serious discernment. But she shies away from people who constantly talk about their miracles or even brag about them. Why? The subject matter is sacred.

"And you know what's interesting? When there's somebody and all they want to do is talk about it, talk about it, talk about it, I tend to doubt the truthfulness of it. I mean, I believe maybe *something* happened. But people are so fundamentally affected by it and it's such a deep, personal, life-changing experience that they become almost more sober. I don't know if it changes you at your core, but it strengthens you at your core . . . you know there are times to talk about it and there are times not to talk about it.

"You don't feel like you've got to convince anybody of anything. That's because it's real. So there are very few times I've actually talked about this. . . . I've talked about it on rare occasions, but only when I've been convinced that it would help somebody . . . it's so special it needs to be valued by the people who hear it. Don't want to give that kind of information to someone who's just going to laugh at Christ. But on the other hand, there are people out there thirsty to know that He's living, He's here with us . . . 'with us to the end of the age.' Well, that means He loves us on a personal level. People always talk about the return of Christ, but I think, 'He's with us. He knows us and He's here somehow.' That's the point."

Therefore, she shares the special moments in her life mentioned above as a sort of testimony.

After all, before her kitchen experience, "I never understood quite the individual level of Christ's love for us . . . not, 'I know your flaws and I know what you're having for dinner!' That's pretty specific. . . . Christ knows you as you; all the little things that make you, you. And He loves us."

Author's note: Betsy holds a bachelor's degree from Agnes Scott College in Decatur, Georgia, and is an M.A.T. student at Converse College in Spartanburg, South Carolina. She and her family are members of a Presbyterian (USA) church in Greenville.

16

Mother Smiles from Heaven

It is hard to live almost a century without seeing a few wonders sprinkled here and there. Lillie Ripley Henderson Craig knows that to be true.

Now ninety-three and widowed but with few health problems, Lillie has lived a blessed life but also a conventional one, a life full of common sense and steadfast service. Ordinarily she shrinks from the miraculous; in fact, Lillie avoids even talking about unusual things, satisfied as she is with her daily bread and the solid evidence of faith and works. But after a long span of living and working and moving about South Carolina, there have been a few otherworldly events. Yes, Lillie admits to two special moments when God communicated in original ways.

The first occurred in the 1970s. How very busy those years were. Lillie was a wife and mother living with husband Edward and her children in the geographical heart of South Carolina. And one day something out of the ordinary happened.

"I was getting ready to drive up in my driveway at my home in Columbia, and in the windshield there was a picture, definitely an outline of my mother's face up in the air. It was right on the outside of the windshield—a reflection of my mother's face. She was smiling. She had a very sweet and happy smile."

Lillie's bright blue eyes grow wide at the telling, even now, since Mother had died four decades earlier, in 1933, during the Great Depression.

What a tranquil look was on that lovely face. The image soothed Lillie, since the mother and daughter had been so close. Lillie missed her presence still.

"Our mother died when we were young, and I was the oldest—nineteen," she says. At that time Lillie's family had moved to Aiken, South Carolina, having recently lost their family home and an insurance business in Columbia. Times were hard. So after her mother's demise, Lillie quickly stepped into a maternal role to help her exhausted, financially struggling father raise three younger brothers.

These memories rushed in through the car windshield that day in 1973.

But no sooner had the vision appeared than it vanished. And there was Lillie, sitting in her car on a street in Columbia. "And I drove on up in the driveway and I went in to my house and the phone was ringing."

Soon she understood what the recent vision meant.

When Lillie picked up the phone, it was her oldest brother, Dan Henderson. He was one of the brothers she had helped raise and later prayed earnestly for during World War II when he was wounded while in the Army.

Dan had bad news about his infant daughter, eighteen months old.

"And he was crying over the phone. He was a man in his early forties, then. And he said, 'Lillie, I just lost my little baby girl.' She was his fourth baby girl. And I said, 'Dan, I'll be right up, I'll come on up to Spartanburg as soon as I can.' And he said, 'Please come.'"

The recent imprint of their mother's face resurfaced in Lillie's mind.

"I went right up to Spartanburg and told Dan about it. But I had also told him over the phone that very day. I said, 'Dan . . . ,' and he was just crying. "I said, 'Dan, now darling, I felt that something had happened. Mother's smiling face had just appeared to me in the windshield of my car."

64

Ultimately, Lillie's glimpse of their mother's face eased Dan's grief in losing his little daughter. He understood the heavenly connection.

As to why their mother was smiling that day, Lillie has no doubt. She smiles broadly herself, leans forward, and says, "Because that baby was *there with her!* She was so happy to have that baby. She *loved* babies and she was a devoted mother."

17

A Special Good-Bye in Aiken

Lillie Craig of the previous chapter received a second supernatural comfort just after her middle brother, Frampton, fifty-two, died of a heart attack in the 1980s. It was the day of his funeral in Aiken. After church, many people milled about the parlor and dining room of his spacious southern home.

"Luncheon was being served and I was standing by the table, helping myself to something, and this young man stood by me and said, 'Somebody out in the hall wants to see you.' And I had never seen this man and I just assumed he was a friend of Frampton's that I did not know. So I said 'thank you' and I put my plate down and went out there, and there was nobody in the hall. The hall was large, a big, wide hall, and the stairway ran up this way about fifteen to twenty steps and then there was a long landing and a few other steps to the rest of the upstairs."

Lillie was rather confused at this point. What was going on and why?

"And I looked and there was Frampton, just the outline of his body. It wasn't a solid body. It was an outline, and he raised his hand to me. I had not seen him for some weeks before he died. He passed away the night before, but I was not there.

"He raised his hand to. . . . He was telling me good-bye."

Frampton had been a tall man, and his figure was totally recognizable. "Definitely, certainly, I could see the expression on his face. . . . I could see he was maybe smiling or something. And then he was gone," says Lillie.

This was Lillie's final good-bye to Brother Framp, but not the first. . . .

Years before, as a Marine volunteer in World War II, he had fought on Iwo Jima, where a foxhole grenade exploded, killing all but him. Framp's unresponsive body was onboard ship en route to the States when a medical staff person passing through the lines of presumed dead saw him blink and realized the young Marine was still alive. Crewmen hurriedly moved the miraculous survivor to the deck and telegraphed home the good news—an answered prayer for Lillie and her family.

Not everyone gets a dramatic good-bye wave like Lillie did, and she knows it. Even today, Framp's poignant farewell from the banister of the Old South staircase sustains her soul. She believes that this parting gesture gave her rest in the midst of great sorrow.

"Oh yes, because I feel like it was a gift from God."

Author's note: Great-grandmother Lillie has seen evidence of a guardian angel on at least one other occasion, while traveling in London, England. Today she attends church regularly while living with her daughter, a son-in-law, and a dog named Darby in Greer, South Carolina.

18

Waves of Mercy
Man Cancer-Free after "Electricity" of All-Night Prayers

Certain dates are carved in the granite of one's mind.

"My name is Jim Allison and I was healed fully and completely of cancer April 11, 1997. I was diagnosed July 17, 1996, with stage 3 testicular cancer."

Thus began a phone interview with a Garden City Beach REALTOR who had cancer as a young married man in his mid-twenties.

From the very first hour the disease was discovered, help of all kinds arrived. Jim categorically states that this chain of compassionate events was miraculous in and of itself. The way people dropped into his life is as amazing as the physical healing that followed. Friends delivered home-cooked meals like clockwork to the house and prayed in organized teams for Jim and his wife, Larissa. He received top-flight, upbeat medical care and treatment in both South Carolina and the Midwest. His employer at the time made gracious accommodations. Churches supported the couple. The beach community even backed Jim in a radio fund-raiser.

This complex interplay of Divine maneuvers finally culminated in two healing services in one eventful week. These were the first healing services Jim had ever attended, and he links the two in terms of his ultimate physical restoration. One healing service took place on a Wednesday morning at his local church in Pawleys Island. Then, three days later, Jim experienced a spectacular, definitive, instantaneous eradication of cancer during a through-the-night prayer and worship session at a large church in Charlotte, North Carolina.

To this day, Jim is without cancer and gloriously grateful. "The Lord declared me cancer-free," he says.

Bad News Deals Hard Blow

His story starts in May 1996. At that time Jim went for a checkup and received antibiotics for what he and the doctor initially thought was a lingering cold or bronchitis. Then persistent wheezing and coughed-up blood pointed to trouble. As matters worsened, an X-ray and blood work indicated a far more sinister diagnosis: testicular cancer.

"What a shocker. At the time I was twenty-six years old and newly married, about a year and a half, and we were trying to start a family. It was a real kick in the teeth. We just were at a loss, didn't know what to do. And this 'certainly isn't something that happens to a twenty-six-year-old.' And this is where the miracles began, the small things, God's provision for us."

Jim and Larissa were thunderstruck at the news, yes. But they marveled at the immediate, rapid confirmations of God's presence. One after another, "gifts" rolled in.

For instance, a nurse on the diagnostic team instantly proclaimed that her husband "had beaten the same thing." How timely, for this was her very first week at the doctor's office. "She knew a lot about it and shortcuts and life after it. She said, 'You need to think about your life after this cancer.' That was huge, and we did," says Jim.

At the nurse's suggestion, the couple underwent sperm banking prior to Jim's surgery to remove the original cancerous tumor. In addition, because of her husband's recent experience, the nurse was able to fast-track the patient to one of the top testicular cancer specialists in the United States, located in Indianapolis, "one of the premier locations in the world for testicular cancer research and treatment," Jim says.

69

Another provision involved finances. "And at that time in our careers, money was tight," says Jim.

But no problem: Friends at a coastal television station presented Jim and Larissa with airplane tickets to fly from Myrtle Beach to Chicago. There, a Pawleys Island youth pastor-friend who was visiting family in the Windy City loaned the Allisons his car to use for the entire time they were in the area. "It was all providentially mapped out—absolutely," says Jim.

That same friend drove the couple to the furnished apartment of a youth minister who was out of town on a mission trip. The young man had offered his place for their lodging. The next day, Jim and his wife sped through Indiana cornfields to another "friend of a friend" in Indianapolis, where they enjoyed dinner and stayed overnight—again, all free and set up by others.

The medical specialist was excellent, personable, and positive, setting a course of maximum-recommended chemotherapy. "We left there very encouraged, excited," remembers Jim. And this was the optimum state of mind to be in, because at that point Jim was quite sick. He had not only lost a great deal of weight, but was wheezing and coughing up blood because the cancer had metastasized into his lungs.

Even so, abundant kindness poured in as they drove back to Chicago. "To cap off this first series of all these things that were provided for us, we were given tickets to the Chicago Cubs at Wrigley Field as a gift from an unknown person. Friends took us out for a Chicago pizza after the game and we flew back to Myrtle Beach the next day."

During the entire trip, they spent very little money.

Chemo Bombs Cancer

Help continued once the couple landed in South Carolina. They headed straight to Jim's local oncologist, who had the prescribed drugs waiting: chemo to target the lungs and other parts of the body that were affected.

Meanwhile, their Bible study supper group from the church they attended at the time spearheaded meals four nights a week. The company Jim then worked for provided one meal per week, and his sister's firm brought food the sixth night. The seventh night consisted of leftovers. "We had a refrigerator full of cakes and pies. We were provided for so generously," says Jim, who up until the time of his illness had prepared all the couple's meals himself.

More assistance came in the form of a local attorney. He showed Jim how to navigate through complicated insurance forms and medical bills. And as another help, at the onset of Jim's chemotherapy, Larissa's boss transferred her office to the Allisons' home—complete with computer, fax machine, and equipment. To top it off, says Jim, a beach-area radio station where Jim had formerly worked put together a fund-raiser at a local establishment. A national musical act performed gratis—raising approximately $5,550 in donations to allay medical expenses.

And so on and so on. "Every need provided—just all of it," recalls Jim.

Meanwhile, Jim endured four grueling cycles of chemo, each lasting four weeks. He shaved his head as hair began to fall out. Nausea began in earnest. His company allowed him to re-arrange and reduce work hours and still keep insurance. "I would literally close my office door and lay down on the floor with a garbage can and get sick."

In November of 1996 Jim returned to Indianapolis for a three-dimensional CT scan. "Physically I was a mess because of the chemotherapy, but a lot of the cancer was arrested. The cancer was controlled . . . but they still found tumors that were active in my lungs. They had to physically cut tumors from my lungs."

This is how he and Larissa spent Thanksgiving. Migraines began after Christmas and on into 1997. Also, he says, "my speech would come out funny."

In spite of all this, the Allisons had jumped back in as church youth leaders, and in March they chaperoned a ski trip to West

Virginia. But a few days later, back in South Carolina, a tumor ruptured in Jim's brain and he began to vomit. Larissa drove him to the hospital in the middle of the night and he had emergency brain surgery to remove the tumor.

This was an extremely dangerous time in every way. Jim resumed chemo and also began full-brain radiation directed out of Indianapolis. Halfway through the treatment, his immune system crashed and he was quarantined to the house. "I could have got a common cold and it could have killed me," he observes.

As this was going on, family and friends throughout the nation continued to pray. It was at Jim's low point that a family member again suggested attending an extended nighttime service—10 p.m. until 6 a.m.—at All Nations Church and Healing Center in Charlotte. (The multi-national full gospel church has since moved to Fort Mill, South Carolina.)

Jim and Larissa had already been reading about healing miracles. They had studied a famous preacher of the past who was greatly anointed for this kind of ministry. They had absorbed various firsthand healing accounts based on prayer. So at this juncture they felt directed to try the setting of a healing service, starting with All Saints Church in Pawleys Island, "where others have also been healed," says Jim. They also prepared to go to the all-night service in Charlotte later that week.

The local service "absolutely was part of the healing process" and educative to them leading up to the Charlotte experience, says Jim. "It was a step that God provided for us to allow us to be able to handle Friday night."

Jim had been reared in an evangelical Lutheran church that did not have a charismatic worship style. In fact, healing services of any kind were new territory for him. Nevertheless, he consented to ride to Charlotte with his family in the back of a van. "I was a little bit begrudging. I was sick. My white blood cell count was through the roof. My tumor markers were terribly high. I was filled with cancer. I was wiped out."

The corporate prophetic prayer at All Nations Church and Healing Center was intense for a neophyte such as Jim. Founders/senior pastors Dr. Mahesh Chavda and his wife, Dr. Bonnie Chavda, were there. Jim recalls that just after midnight Dr. Bonnie Chavda stopped her husband from speaking and said, "There's a man from the beach who is sick and needs to come forward." So, with trepidation Jim, Larissa, and her parents moved to the front of the church. Meanwhile, church leaders were summoned forward to lay hands on Jim and begin to intercede on his behalf for healing.

Jim travels back in his mind to this emotional experience. He says, "Some prayed in tongues and some prayed in English. And eventually I was so exhausted that they kind of eased me to the floor and continued to pray. And like a bolt of lightning, it ran through my feet—this electricity, just supernatural—ran from my feet to the top of my head. And the words, 'It is done, it is done, it is done, it is done,' came to me in an interior fashion. And they were quickly replaced by the words 'Thank you, Jesus. Thank you, Jesus. Thank you, Jesus" over and over and over in my head. Not ten times, not a hundred times, but a thousand times. And one of the men at this church said, 'You've been healed!' and I said, 'I know I have been.' And we were so tired and they helped me up off the ground. And they said, 'Go and live!' And we did."

Go and Live!

Utterly drained, the family stayed that night in a Charlotte motel and returned home Saturday. On Monday, Jim went directly to see his radiologist and oncologist. These people were friends by now, folks he knew well and had seen five days a week during rigorous treatment.

"The nurses, they said, 'We've heard about this before. We believe this. We know people who have been healed.' So I had my blood done and they rushed the results through and I didn't have a drop of cancer in my body. Friday afternoon I was filled with cancer. Tumor markers were off the charts. Monday morning, I didn't have any at all. And I was healed that night. I was healed April 11, 1997."

Once the chemo cycled out of Jim's system, "I got my strength back, I got my hair back, I resumed my life and re-built and—by the grace of God—got everything back into place."

But there was further restoration. He and his wife began the invitro fertilization process. At first it failed. But during this setback, Larissa began a children's ministry at a local children's hospital that provided free books and toys every Thursday except Thanksgiving. This program served over twenty-five thousand families, says Jim.

"And that was sort of the thing between the cancer—and our children! And we now have two beautiful children—a little boy and a little girl that were born through invitro, twins born twenty-one months apart."

19

Prayer Book Fragment Survives Katrina

Tommy Moore marvels at "the number of things that had to come together" to preserve the three-by-five-inch relic he found in the rubble of St. Bernard Parish following the most devastating hurricane in U.S. history. He and a mission team from Simpsonville, South Carolina, had traveled to just outside the Ninth Ward of New Orleans to help. Though the flood had receded months earlier, the area was still deserted. The three weeks it had spent under water had made it a wasteland. Far into the distance, empty businesses and random debris marred the landscape. Skeletal house frames leaned precariously. Bugs crawled everywhere, as if they owned the place. St. Bernard had taken a hard beating from post-Hurricane Katrina flooding.

When Tommy arrived along with a crew from his family's home church, Advent United Methodist, the group faced a decision—whether or not to try to salvage a badly damaged home owned by a disabled man. Frankly, the volunteers from Advent were weighing sad options: Was there any potential in this mess? Should they even attempt to redeem what was left of this old house? Or should they move on to more promising projects to better use their time and strength?

By far, the most compelling reason to keep working on the house was the homeowner. He was an easygoing man with severe diabetes and a paralyzed left hand and foot. His mother had died only one year earlier, leaving the property to him. With just one good arm and foot, he had already managed to resurrect many of the original floor planks by yanking out nails and hauling boards into one room.

"This is all I've got in the world," he had told Tommy and the others, recalling how he had jokingly told his mother before her death, "Now that you're leaving me the house, 'the Big One' will probably come." (And sure enough, Katrina did, wiping out communities, legacies, and dreams in a maelstrom that made history.) He added, "Well, even before the storm I never was attached to anything, and I always knew Who to trust in."

These words pushed the group forward. "But I think if it hadn't been for his determination," says Tommy, the South Carolina group would have chosen a more stable structure to save.

Now up for the challenge, the team began its house rescue. Tommy found himself trying to make order out of chaos in one of the darkened, ruined rooms that had been submerged up to the ceiling for weeks. Every few minutes he would bump into a trash can jammed with wood and refuse.

"There was no electricity and all the windows had this nasty film on them," he says. Volunteers worked waist-deep in dried-out junk. They privately wondered if this was God's particular will for the trip.

Then suddenly "this piece of wood fell toward me at eye level, and this piece of paper was laminated to the board. I took it outside and I couldn't believe my eyes," says Tommy. Before him was a wooden slab with words "affixed to a board" by weeks of flooding. It was an old prayer. The title: "Advent Prayer."

"I read it and I was just stunned by the words. We were just in awe."

The homeowner came over, saw the remarkable find, and exclaimed, 'This was the first prayer in my mom's prayer book. As long as I can remember, she had a prayer book by the table."

The fact that they found this keepsake at all was incredible to everyone. Workers, dirty from their labors, walked over to take a look.

But another astounding realization was this: the name "*Advent* Prayer."

And what's more, the favorite old prayer mentioned "the struggling and the needy," as well as "words of encouragement for those who despair." These were precisely the hurting people *Advent* United Methodist had come to aid in their time of need.

Tommy says, "We had to pause and marvel at the miracle of this one piece of paper surviving volumes of water and being found nineteen months later by us, a group from Advent, six hundred miles away, who were there simply to help. What a powerful lesson. We completely sheetrocked the house. You would have never convinced me in a million years that we could have done that in one week's work."

Author's note: Also among the flood wreckage the team rescued a velour "Jesus in the Garden of Gethsemane" tapestry with no trace of damage after weeks under muddy water. "It was in perfect condition," says Tommy. St. Bernard was his second Katrina mission trip in only three weeks. The first was with a Christian student group from Furman University that worked in Pass Christian, Mississippi. In the workday world, Tommy is a strategic planner for individuals and organizations.

20

God Talk at the Kitchen Table

Nearing ninety and the end of her life, my friend Andigoni Gallani Muzekari began to mention clusters of healing miracles that occurred in time-worn Albania when she was a girl. As her eyes dimmed, she recalled those long-ago events in a faraway cathedral with inner clarity and breathless wonder.

It all happened in her own hometown, she maintained. "They had the faith," she said, smiling and nodding in agreement with a voice deep inside. The faith to accept God's acts simply, just as they appeared.

Now, almost a century later, Mrs. Muzekari drew word portraits of the land of her childhood: distant Albania, so ruggedly beautiful to the eye but so crushed by centuries of suffering. Commoners and notables alike shared the region's native soil of deep childhood faith. (Four years before Mrs. Muzekari's birth, Mother Teresa was born to Albanian parents in present-day Macedonia.)

For centuries upon centuries, Albania endured isolation, poverty, pestilence, feudal wars, dictators, purges, tribunals, and other political repressions. These catastrophic events piled up a painful past—heavy stone upon heavy stone—even before the invasion by Italian strongman Benito Mussolini on the cusp of World War II.

Old Friends Sipping Tea

Mrs. Muzekari and I were former neighbors in the historic Earle Street part of downtown Greenville. Back in the 1980s she was a recent widow who babysat our children. She pushed their strollers to the park and served homemade chicken soup when they were sick. Our friendship was a funny one, and we laughed as we navigated through Albanian/southern accents and a forty-year age difference.

Years passed, but from time to time Mrs. Muzekari would invite me back downtown into the sunny kitchen of her pretty, old brick house for breakfast or lunch. Sometimes her sister-in-law up the block would join us. She too was a proud Albanian American and great cook. Muzekari dishes steamed hot and fragrant with oregano fresh from the garden. At noon there were platters of orzo pasta, stuffed grape leaves, moussaka, baked chicken, lentil soup, cold couscous with lemon and parsley, all finished off with baklava and hot tea or coffee.

Without fail, a cheery flower vase smiled up from her Formica table. Always-spotless, her crisp, white curtains fluttered in windows that were cracked just enough to let in fresh air. She believed devoutly in cleaning, ironing, and re-hanging all curtains every spring, "old country" Albanian-style.

So, with our hot mugs poured full, we would discuss food, family, faith—and the supernatural. We talked about how God worked in shocking ways long ago, and nowadays, too, always maintaining a gentle theological arrangement. The meal finally spread out, she would pronounce, "We're ready!" and then grab my hand while I prayed over our food in "the Methodist way" and she crossed herself. Invariably, she would share some fact from a saint or feast day derived from the Orthodox wall calendar from Saint George Greek Orthodox Cathedral, or maybe even a word about Christ Church Episcopal; occasionally, I'd enjoy a peak at her icon collection, always candle-lit and luminous in a dark, home-style altar.

Year followed year like the pendulum of a familiar chiming clock. Mrs. Muzekari's manner and conversation deepened. She wore a cross necklace all the time now, not just on special occasions. She began to tell the "cathedral story" repeatedly. And at each telling, her face shown with the memory of when God had reached down to her Albanian neighbors with his very own hands to heal desperately ill children. Was she now, in her late eighties and with her heart failing, thinking of herself as a child who God would soon visit and make whole again?

Mounted on the kitchen wall was an old Berat tambourine, painted with a scene of the city. Beside it, other relics. She referred to these often.

Questions Unanswered

If only I had inquired more about Mrs. Muzekari's girlhood in the walled-fortress hometown of Berat, a settlement that pre-dated Christ and extended back twenty-four hundred years. There, close-knit villagers drew water from wells. Her father owned a farming estate of vineyards and herds that provided relative prosperity for the family.

Also, I should have unearthed details about the city cathedral, the one she mentioned again and again, as in a waking vision. This house of worship consecrated to St. Elijah the Prophet towered over an already church-filled community. Even today, Berat is called "the town of a thousand windows."

Mrs. Muzekari insisted that the cathedral had earned its well-founded reputation for Divine encounters down through the years. She credited this to the people's widespread belief, which created a climate conducive to supernatural intervention. The word of God's Favor drew a steady flow of people from hamlets in the surrounding countryside. That is, before that noble sanctuary was desecrated and burned to the ground by Communists and invaders in the chaotic years after World War II.

Did Mrs. Muzekari or her family actually witness the amazing cathedral cures she relived at her kitchen table? Or did she just hear about them from stunned parents who left the sacred spot with their children suddenly whole and well? Did some of her own relatives receive a touch from God? She spoke as if everyone did.

I should have found out more, but didn't; instead, I simply soaked in the age-old memories, assuming—wrongly—that her stories would last forever. And so would she.

Treading through Tragic Years

Mrs. Muzekari explained how the Communists eventually seized her father's holdings, tormented the citizens, and burned down the cathedral—and many places like it—after their ruthless takeover in 1945. They closed all the churches, persecuted Christians, and destroyed almost all she had known and loved. Atheism stamped its face on the people and the land. The Albanians were forced to hide their faith in public.

Fortunately, she never witnessed these atrocities: she married an Albanian American and came to the United States by way of Ellis Island in 1934. Once in Greenville, she and her husband raised four children and sank deep roots into the community.

"How I love this country, how I love America," she often murmured.

Yet, the long-ago cathedral vision persisted. When she was young, parents from miles around who lived in grinding poverty would bring their desperately ill and dying children to the cathedral. Devoid of modern medicines and often without doctors of any kind, villagers would climb the steep, jagged hill Berat was erected on, carry the children into the hushed sanctuary, and place them at the altar all night long. Candles burned and prayers went up. It was their only hope, their last hope. Despairing mothers and fathers cried out to God through the dark night for miracle cures. And miracles happened, said Mrs. Muzekari simply. Healings occurred there because the people of that day believed, she said. The little ones who were supposed to fly away as angels didn't. Not then. Instead, they got well. The overjoyed parents would leave something of value at the church—coins, rings, other jewelry or treasured items—in tearful thanks to God. Then they would take their well children back home.

The years took their toll, and Mrs. Muzekari passed from this life to the next in April 2004. She was close to ninety. At the funeral home, friends streamed out the doors and down a long hall to pay respects. A cherished Orthodox icon rested on her chest. In 1978, when she and her elder son returned from a visit with family in Albania, she carefully smuggled this sacred object under her dress past Communist Albanian guards, risking her life to get it to America.

Her funeral service took place in Christ Church Episcopal. That was the location. But in matters of faith, the Albanian girl had returned to a cathedral in Berat for final healing.

21

Churchman Watches Warrior Angel Bless Lake

For the past several years, when October comes I load up the car and drive with one of my lady friends from this Carolina to the other to attend the annual Healing Winds Conference. This gathering at Lake Logan Episcopal Center focuses on healing prayer. It is sponsored by two chapters of the International Order of St. Luke the Physician. The setting is unfailingly serene, except for unannounced gusts of wind that swoop down between the Blue Ridge Mountains. Jewel-tone leaves flicker in the water's reflection. Reverend Turner Guidry of North Carolina says a nearby eleven-mile road winds up to a crest "where you can see all the way into South Carolina." On that slender thread, I include his remarkable account in a book about South Carolina miracles.

While on retreat and his ordinary adventures, Reverend Guidry wears hiking boots, jeans, and the rugged vest of a confirmed outdoorsman. He talks seriously with friends about industrial-sized barbecue grills, prime cuts of meat for smoking, the best available wood (cherry or oak?), and the proper fixin's. Back home in Hayesville, North Carolina, Turner is a middle school counselor with several decades' experience under his belt. He is also a seasoned acoustical guitarist, singer, and youth leader at the Episcopal Church of the Good Shepherd, where he serves as deacon.

Finally, at rock bottom, Turner is a man of deep prayer. But until the fall of 2002, he had never seen anything otherworldly *of any kind*. He had rarely considered the possibility. Things like that happened only to people he knew, or *people he knew about* in devotional classics.

Before the conference began, Turner and two others were in the administration building praying in advance for the lead team and the more than one hundred participants who would arrive in several hours. The group sat in a room with ample windows facing the lake. That day, autumn was dressed up in her very finest clothes and she didn't mind at all showing off those brilliant reds and golds.

"As we were praying aloud and silently for the Lord to provide angels to guard and protect all of Lake Logan during this Healing Winds Conference, immediately as I prayed that, I had a tremendous overwhelming sense of presence," says Turner. "And as I looked out—and also in my mind's eye, it was kind of a combination of the two—I was aware of angels that were standing on the ridge line, all around the edge of the mountains, all around the Blue Ridge Parkway and back down the side of the ridge. And they were huge. They were much, much taller than the trees on the ridge and they were standing like sentries. They were in armor and they were spaced out up there. Then at the dam end of the lake—the far end of the lake from where I was—was an angel that was just immense, straddling with a foot on either side of the dam on the shore there and in armor also, with a sword held in front of him and pointing straight up. As I saw this, he took the sword and laid it down in the lake, with the hilt of the sword being there by the dam and the tip of the sword stretching all the way across the lake.

"The lake is half a mile long, and with the sword, that would make him nearly 5,000 feet tall, somewhere in that neighborhood."

Turner could see to the top of this massive messenger.

"He was in armor with breastplates and armor on his arms and helmet. He laid the sword down and left it down in the lake, and I was aware of it being under the water there. And so I didn't say anything to anybody there. I'd never had an experience like this before. I just was overwhelmed, but I kept it to myself. That was about nine o'clock in the morning, and all through the day I was aware of their presence.

"And as I looked, I could see there was also a shimmering vault, a kind of a net of gold that covered the whole watershed and the lake, kind of a gossamer gold protective shield that was around the place. All through the day and all through the night I was aware of the sentry angels that were there and of the large angel that was at the end of the lake."

The next morning, Turner got up early and went to the dining hall to journal his experience. "I said, 'Lord, what is the meaning of this?' And He said, 'I'm making this place a place of healing and _____ for My people.' [Turner heard an interior Voice but cannot recall the precise word here.] He was explicit about it being a place of healing, whether it was healing and restoration or healing and renewal. I was aware of it all weekend and I mentioned it to [Reverend] John Rice, who was there, and to a couple of other people." Rice serves as rector at Church of the Good Shepherd.

A number of people at the conference asked Turner to share what he had seen, and he did so later that night at a Generational Healing Eucharist Service. This is a special time when worshippers bring their own pre-written family trees to consecrate. They include both the blessings down through the generations and the family difficulties, addictions, and tragedies.

But first, during the daytime teaching, something else happened. During Rice's lecture about "sins unwrapping from us like gauze off of a mummy," Turner was standing in the back of the large, high-arched Celebration Hall where about 130 people were seated, windows all around. And suddenly Turner saw "this gauze visually coming off of people's heads and the sword came out of the lake at that point like right through the middle of the building, right above everybody's heads, and severed that dirty gauze from everybody. And it [the sword] just went on up through the rafters into the air and was gone. It went back to the lake, floated away.

The sword had accomplished this and then just disappeared upward, he explained.

"And then that night, at the Generational Healing Service, when the people brought all their genograms up and put them on the altar, I was assisting John, who was the celebrant. When he was saying a prayer about severing the people from the generations [of sin], the sword came straight down between the altar and the people and, again, severed the people from those bad connections."

Afterward, Turner had not spoken about this latest vision to anybody, "and a woman came up and said, 'Did you see it?' and I said, 'What?' and she said, 'A sword came down between the altar and the people and severed those ties with those negative things on the genograms.' So it was confirmed there."

Two weeks later, Turner returned to Lake Logan for a Cursillo weekend. During the Eucharist, the priest celebrating spoke the familiar liturgical words, "'and with angels and archangels and all the company of heaven . . . ,' and immediately I was aware of the angels' presence in the same way, as sentries around the whole property."

1 Chronicles 21:16a records a parallel image: "David looked up and saw the angel of the Lord standing between heaven and earth, with a drawn sword in his hand extended over Jerusalem."

Johnny Keesee, executive director of Lake Logan Episcopal Center, commented on this chapter, saying: "This is a fascinating piece. I am keenly aware of Lake Logan having a spirit, a peaceful, comfortable, and, most assuredly, a safe spirit about it. I have attributed this sense in part to the intimacy of being cradled between the high peaks, but that doesn't explain the Divine presence one experiences. . . . I personally feel it and know that it's real, and many of the guests have spoken about it, though none as vividly as Turner."

22

Irish Eyes Gaze on the Next World

European barber Martina Hurley beguiles customers with tales about her native Ireland while clipping and styling hair in a popular Greer, South Carolina, shop. Since settling in the United States in 1993, she's lost none of the rhythmic accent, lilting idioms, and narrative flare that make St. Patrick's homeland so enchanting.

One day while she groomed a client, Martina's heart again crossed the Atlantic. This time she replayed the final notes of her dear mother's life. She explained how "Mammy"—as she lovingly called her—"saw people at the end of the bed" prior to her death, and also how several months later—at the very instant of death—sunlight inexplicably pierced the black clouds outside her mother's hospital window in Dublin, fully illuminating the sickroom. This blaze of sunshine tarried three or four minutes during her mother's passage onward, then rapidly withdrew, replaced by darkness the rest of the day.

Such things are but quiet, subtle movements of the spirit, fleeting illuminations. But they console families. Down through the ages, souls near death often issue pronouncements, visitations, dreams, or glimpses of the hereafter. Once these loved ones pass on, relatives and friends sift through the mysterious messages for the rest of their lives.

"As time goes past I do get comfort," admits Martina. "At the beginning I was in shock. You can't believe it. But as time goes by you try to remember. You remember things better because your head is a little bit sharper."

A devoted lifelong Catholic, her mother Florrie Buckley attended Mass weekly with her husband and frequently said nine-day prayer novenas for her three daughters, large extended family, and friends. Spiritually minded, it was natural that Florrie and another daughter would join millions of international pilgrims who yearly visit the healing grotto and basilica at Lourdes, France—even before cancer threw a shadow across Florrie's life. For more than a century and a half, Lourdes has been a sanctuary of penance, conversion, and healing. Tall candles flicker in the cave-like shrine. Supplicants kneel prayerful and weeping.

Later, while battling her own illness in 2004, Florrie returned to Lourdes with the entire family and participated in a torchlight Marian procession that is over a century old. Martina remembers: "She wanted to be healed from all this cancer and never wanted it to come back. Another pilgrim asked her, 'Don't you feel better when you're here?' And she did. She felt great. She looked good. There are pictures at the Grotto of the wheelchairs and the walkers all over the place, people just getting up from their walkers and walking away, healed! And they have a procession . . . and it would put a tear to a stone. Incredible, with their candles . . . , just singing songs. And beds, hospital beds in the procession! There's thousands of people, everybody, anybody can go there, walking around to the Grotto . . . just an incredible place, very holy."

But despite Florrie's second and last visit to Lourdes and a dip in the holy spring, her condition worsened. Next, before her final hospitalization, she and her family traveled to St. Peter's Square on Easter Sunday, April 2005, two weeks before Pope John Paul II died. There they watched the frail pontiff wave from the window of his study. Martina recalls, "There were thousands upon thousands, and many not Catholic. It was very touching. It just amazed me. It sent a shiver up you."

By June, Florrie languished in an imposing old Catholic hospital in Dublin named The Mather. She clearly saw "people at the end of the bed." It was unsettling. The "people" huddled there but wouldn't look up at her. Troubled, the sick woman conferred with an elderly cloistered nun, a childhood friend from her Irish hometown who had entered a local Siena convent as a young girl for life. Only because the sister was hospitalized herself did the two meet and converse.

In her opinion, what did souls gathered at the bottom of the bed mean? The nun's reply: she thought it was a sign of imminent death. "The nun said, 'People do come to you.'" Florrie concealed the significance of this information from her family.

"Mammy couldn't really say who the people were. They had long gray hair and gray clothes and they wouldn't look at her," says Martina. "But the nun later told my sister, 'They weren't ready for your mammy yet. That's why she was here for another little while.'"

Though Martina was certain that the matriarch would recover, she did not. One day at mid-afternoon, with her loved ones alongside her, Florrie died. And exactly at that moment, the dark, slate-gray sky that had been so menacing all day long outside the windows immediately broke open.

"The sun came into the room at three o'clock, through high, long windows because it was an old hospital. And it wasn't even a sunny day outside—the most amazing fact! It was just a kind of dull October day, not a whole lot of sunshine. It was only there for a couple of minutes. Kind of dark, cloudy, overcast. We never really left the hospital till late that night, but you could see out because of all the windows . . . and it remained dark except for that moment. God had come and taken her. For the sun to come in to last only a couple of minutes was kind of a miracle. . . . It was hard at the time to see that, but as months go by now I think of that a lot, because you don't hear that too often."

Author's note: Martina and her husband grew up next door to one another in the same Irish town of Drogheda. They and their daughter frequently entertain family and friends visiting from Ireland, including her dad, who loves to babysit.

23

Charleston Group Awed by Ukrainian Healings

Decades-old arthritis gone and canes tossed away . . . Eyes dimmed by cataracts made new . . . Depression banished . . . Chernobyl-induced asthma calmed, with free breathing restored . . . Hearing recovered . . . All this and more have happened when Charleston church members prayed with hurting people in a foreign land. Many of the changes were instantaneous.

"We have hundreds of stories we could tell you! When you get to the Ukraine, you have to 'put your seatbelt on'" to absorb the number of supernatural healings, says Johnnie Corbett of Johns Island, South Carolina. For several years, he and wife, Jean, have led mission teams from St. Michael's Episcopal Church in Charleston to the small rural villages surrounding the city of Zhitomir, Ukraine. The couple recruits, organizes, and trains teams, and later teaches alongside South Carolina friends upon arrival in this former Soviet country.

"Miracle after miracle was happening," says Johnnie. "Your faith just builds and you've seen God working. You're just standing back. You're just an instrument of His. You say, 'God, I don't deserve to be in this position.' People with headaches have had the headaches for years. The medication given to them by the doctors only dulls the pain but does not heal them. And you pray for them and the people say, 'It's gone! It's gone!' Just all kinds of things are happening. When you lay hands on a goiter on somebody's neck about the size of a tennis ball and begin to pray, and you feel your hand go down and you move your hand—and it's gone. That blows you away!"

St. Michael's is downtown Charleston's oldest church building, dating from 1751. George Washington and other notables have worshipped in its latched, wood-box pews. The massive white-columned entrance presides over the intersection of Broad and Meeting streets, known as The Four Corners of Law for its strategic juxtaposition of civic and religious structures. The 186-foot church steeple regards the carriages ambling down shady avenues nearby and the Charleston Harbor beyond.

The congregation believes that God heals through prayer. It extends this conviction by sending teams overseas. Jean herself has trained healing-prayer groups for decades, assisting the rector for twenty years until her retirement in December 2007. As of fall 2007, the congregation had backed four teams to the Ukraine alone, each averaging twelve U.S. team members. The goals: to teach Ukrainians in many small Baptist churches in poor, rural villages ten to a hundred miles from Zhitomir how to pray biblically for healing, to demonstrate participatory healing services, to deliver food to the abject poor scattered throughout the rural terrain, and to import dental care.

These South Carolinian missionaries are mindful that the Ukraine is just emerging from rulers opposed to belief in God: first, oppression by czarist Russia; then the strong arms of Communist Russia, Nazi Germany, and the U.S.S.R. "But now God is moving in miraculous ways," explains Johnnie. "When we come back and share the stories [in Charleston and beyond], we have people so excited they line up and they want to go with us."

Here the couple shares Divine interventions from 2004:

An arthritic woman could not harvest her garden—her only food supply—because of gnarled, arthritic hands. She lived alone. Her fingers were swollen and she could not bend them. Tears streamed down her face. From antiquity, older ladies such as herself have worn headscarves and are referred to as "babushkas." As the teams laid hands on her and prayed, Johnnie felt the swollen hands literally reduce in size. "I felt her hands going down. I moved my hand and looked and the swelling was gone. She exclaimed, 'Now I can harvest my food!'" And Johnnie started weeping along with her. He does so even now, recalling her joy.

Arthritis is prevalent in the Ukraine, says Jean. One older lady walked with two sticks cut from trees. As a St. Michael's team ministered to her inside the village church, she fixed her eyes on the ceiling and yellow stained-glass windows. Suddenly, as the group prayed for her—a few with hands on her knees—the translator exclaimed, "She sees light." Jean says, "Apparently she had cataracts and so she couldn't see. So, we were praying for her knees. Her knees get better—but her eyes were opened." The lady had died by the next year's mission trip, "but she died with the ability to see."

Another woman came with a fire-engine red face due to high blood pressure. After prayer, "her face lightened up," says Jean. "She felt so good, she stayed and ate lunch with us, then returned for the rest of the conference that day and, I think, the whole next day. And God just zapped her." Her health improved to the extent that she joined the work team to prepare meals and brought family members to church. That type of physical-spiritual turnaround was common, says Jean.

She describes "one dear, dear lady with thick glasses. We prayed for healing of her knees. She went home and the next morning when she got up, apparently she was just completely healed and she put her stick down. She'd been walking with the aid of a stick for twenty or more years. And she went out in her garden, picked a big bouquet of white chrysanthemums and zinnia flowers, and brought it to the church. As she was walking—down that old village dirt road full of pot holes—her neighbors came out and called to her, 'Luba, where's your stick?' and she said, 'God has healed me and I'm taking flowers to the church.' The second year we were there she showed up again with two hands wrapped around another bouquet of flowers, and still no stick."

During a teaching conference with about seventy-five locals, Jean asked who wanted to come to the front of the church for prayer. Reluctantly, very slowly, a hand finally went up and Jean called forward a wife and mother in her mid-thirties with years of back pain and sleeplessness. At the time, she didn't say that her husband was a pastor who also had many health issues. "The doctors couldn't help her. So I asked her to sit in a little wooden school chair on this tiny little stage where we were teaching. I said, 'We're going to ask Jesus to come and heal her back.'" The lady faced the audience. "As we prayed she started smiling pretty quickly. I asked the translator, 'What is going on with her?' and she replied, 'She said she's healed.' The team prayed for another minute. She was about to get out of the chair and she's beaming. She stood up and told the congregation that all the pain was gone. And she moved and she wiggled and she went back to her pew and sat down beaming with joy." When the team asked for one more volunteer, the entire congregation got up at once and pushed forward, trying to get into that chair, "with their canes, their sticks, their wobbling, bumping into each other."

In the village, Johnnie met a Chernobyl survivor. This older woman suffered with asthma, diabetes, high blood pressure, and other problems. She had endured the explosion and evacuation. "And all of a sudden she looked at me and her eyes got big. And she said when she was taking her nap [that day], 'God showed me you in my dream, that you were bringing me a gift.' We talked with her, gave her a bag of groceries, and asked if she would like prayer. She said, 'Yes,' and we prayed with her. And just after a minute or two, she said, 'I can breathe! I can breathe!' Before prayers she could hardly walk because of difficulty breathing and arthritic knees and joints. After prayers she started bouncing around and so I knew God had not only healed her breathing, but healed her arthritis, too, and anything else maybe that was on the inside of her. Actually, she went out the door and out into the yard and started running around and praising God. God restored her lungs completely . . . and when we left her house and went back up that hill, she came with us, beating on her chest, saying, 'Praise God, Praise God, Praise God.' And you leave there and you say, 'Wow!' I mean, this was a woman who could not walk five steps without having to take a puff on her inhaler."

In the fall of 2007, the Corbetts and thirteen others returned from yet another healing mission to the Ukraine, with similar results. The pastor there wrote back to the United States, "Hundreds of people got healed."

24

A Summons to Seminary
Illumination During a Dark Night of the Soul

It is a weighty matter to decide to attend seminary. Even in college, Trish Gwinn had watched the idea bounce up and down and side to side on the waves of her conscious and unconscious mind. Years passed, and "the call" sank almost entirely; then bobbed up to the surface again.

By the spring of 2002, this wife and mother was approaching forty and still struggling with an inclination to go to seminary. Where should she study? When? How? Deeper she plunged, exploring the notion with church-going family, friends, casual acquaintances, and officials alike. Trish prodded the topic with prayer. She began a more systematic, biblical study of the Holy Spirit than she had ever attempted before.

"My understanding did increase," she reflects.

The pull continued, irresistible.

During this seminal period in her life Trish and McCrady Gwinn's only child, Claudia, then seven, was having severe migraines, despite many treatments and ongoing medical attention.

"I have never worried about one thing and one person so much in my entire life," writes Trish about that time. "I love her with all that I am. I would suffer for her if only I could. I would take away this pain and leave her well if it were within my power to do so. I adore her. I think she is a magnificent person. I cannot begin to express the depth of my love for her."

In June 2002, a vision occurred to Trish during one of Claudia's many headaches. Trish reconstructed it later in her own words and at her mother's urging. "I was wide awake," she says of the scene. "Time was lost." Three minutes seemed like thirty minutes; thirty minutes melted into a mere three.

The following was written in January 2003, with a few passages removed to focus on the event at hand:

"I write this in completely sound mind and body. I have hesitated to write it for so long for several reasons. First, is the belief that it is not something I will ever forget. Second, is the knowledge that mere words, or at least my mere words, cannot begin to adequately describe the moment. At the encouragement of Mother, I put down these thoughts.

"On Saturday evening or I suppose Sunday a.m. . . . is really where it all begins. Claudia woke up with a migraine in the middle of the night—this is completely different than any other time. I gave her two medicines and nothing seemed to be working. She tossed and turned and cried and my heart broke. I lay down in the bed with her. She allowed me to stroke her temple—something she had never let me do before. I began to pray for the Holy Spirit to come upon her, to take this pain away for tonight—not forever—just give her rest for this night. I was so afraid I had given her the wrong combination of medicine—I was adrift and did not know what else to do. I prayed and I prayed fervently.

"I said things such as: 'I believe the Holy Spirit can give her rest, please come' repeatedly. I was lying on my right side with Claudia spooned against me in my arms and I felt the presence of evil crawling up my back. It was black and cold, wet and slimy. [Later, Trish described it as a long snake crawling up her back and down her neck.] I said, 'Get behind me Satan, I believe in the Holy Spirit,' and he was gone in a moment, an absolute blink of an eye. That horrible, cold, creepy feeling vanished.

"And in the next heartbeat, at the end of the bed appeared the Holy Spirit and with Him God the Father and the Lord Jesus Christ. They were in the room at the foot of the bed. Claudia was quiet and still and asleep and They/He were present.

96

"It was as if a veil covered Their faces. The air looked changed in some way—but difficult to describe. It is so easy to see in my mind's eye and so impossible to capture on paper. It was almost as if it was mist—sort of light blue mist with the essence of light within it. This I believe is what I actually perceived as a veil. Yet there were distinctly three presences. The divine Trinity.

"The feeling of beauty and love was overpowering. I was completely humbled—but not in a bad or fearful way. There was no fear in this place. What fear had been there had been vanquished by this holy presence. I was overcome by God's love and beauty. I began to pray and worship. Tears streamed down my face. I praised God unendingly, almost unconsciously of my free will. I was overcome with devotion. I prayed to the Father as one—not to all three separate—and no longer to the Holy Spirit but to the Father. And I had certain understanding, given to me by Him, that this was appropriate.

"While I praised, Claudia stirred and rolled over, face into my arms and breast. I said something like, 'O Father, this is how you love me,' and He said three times: 'you understand, you understand, you understand.' I understood in that moment that God loves His people like we love our children: with all our heart. They disappoint us, they are disobedient to us, they make mistakes and we forgive them, yet through it all we would not let go of them for anything. We love them. We want them to do well and be happy. We are so proud and thrilled for them when they do well, when they choose well. God loves us like this. I knew it in that moment. I will know this comfort forever.

"Then I looked toward the Holy Spirit, and I know full well He put the question in my heart. I said, 'Do I go to school?' and He replied three times: 'Go to school, go to school, go to school.' I said: 'Yes, Lord.'

"I continued praising and I could not look at the end of the bed for long. I could not fix a steady gaze upon the presence of God. He demanded by His very being a bowed head. I looked at Claudia's head nestled in my arms. I was saying: 'I praise you with the roar of volcanoes' (I remember saying that distinctly) when I noticed a dark blue light shining on her temple. I then said: 'I praise you with angels and archangels, with Seraphim and . . . ' I could not remember Cherubim for the life of me and then I did and it was if the whole room opened up. As if a curtain was torn wide open and I was surrounded by indigo blue sky, with ivory iridescent clouds in the background. I stood in the midst of this. The room, Claudia, the bed—all was gone. It was I looking into this vast expanse—this endless blue space. This was a vision; I know it as sure truth.

"There was an angel in the background. She stood with her feathered wings folded and I looked at her as from the side. I heard a voice—God's voice. He was with me at my side yet unseeable to me. I was so focused on that angel and sky."

Here, the Voice instructed Trish with a comforting message. Then later, "The angel was back and her wings caught warm and beautiful light (not fire, but burning peaceful light), and it consumed the angel and she was gone. The curtain closed and I was in the bed with Claudia in my arms, and the Trinity at the end of the bed."

And Trish heard again—three times—a peaceful message. Her account continues: "Claudia began to grow restless now and rolled away from me on the bed. I began praising again and knew (just with some understanding) that I should go, and yet Claudia seemed restless and I could not bring myself to leave her, and more importantly leave this Almighty Presence. The Lord said to me three times: 'Rise and go.' I said: 'I trust you Lord, I go.' And I left her room and went to my bed.

"I tire now. This was the single most incredible experience of my life. I think on it every day without fail. McCrady said to me when I told him about it that it was 'a blessing.' Of that he is right. It was a blessing given to me by the Holy Spirit. My faith, so very little, had nothing to do with it. God reached out and spoke to me and my life is forever changed. He came to me that night for whatever purpose He wanted to. He arranged all things for it to happen. I always knew God existed, but I know with an absolute and unshakeable certainty now. Truly, Jesus was so right when he told Thomas how good are those who believe and have never seen . . . I go to school now. I have no idea where I am going, but I know I am going with God and that is all that really matters.

"God is sovereign and almighty. He is the Living God. All things do work through Him and because of Him. Believe and know the comfort of the Spirit—the assurance of the risen Christ. Believe in Him, and if you cannot bring yourself to believe in what appears to human eyes as invisible mystery—then look at me, and know I speak the truth. I have seen Him and He is and He loves you."

Author's note: Trish drives from her home in Greenville to Erskine Theological Seminary, where she is in the midst of her course of studies. She feels called to some aspect of pastoral ministry. The family belongs to a local Presbyterian (USA) church.

25

Snapshots of God

These "brief witnesses" by parishioners appear in handouts at St. Michael's Episcopal Church in Charleston and are used with permission.

Give It God's Way

Two members of a prayer group I was in prayed about serious financial problems. About that time, I received an unexpected gift of $100. It was a lot of money for me.

God put one of our needy group members on my heart and led me to send the $100 as an anonymous gift. The money didn't solve his problem, but gave great encouragement. Later I received six more unexpected gifts, each for $100. Pleased with this result, I decided to send $100 to the other needy group member. He was hurt by what he referred to as "charity," and I felt badly.

I realized that giving led by God, with no thought of return, brings blessing to the giver as well as the recipient. Giving on my own, with hope of gain, blesses neither me nor the one I tried to help.

—Reverend Richard Belser, Rector (now retired)
St. Michael's, August 2001

Hearts of Stone and Flesh

In 1979 I attended an Episcopal Cursillo retreat at Camp St. Christopher. I was angry with a friend and I didn't know how to forgive or reconcile the issue.

During the weekend, I sat alone on the porch overlooking the ocean. I wanted God to give me a clean heart and so I prayed, "Lord, have mercy." Jesus showed himself to me with his arms stretched out on a cross and he looked at me with eyes of love. I saw myself standing by him holding my large, black, stony heart in my arms. He told me to give it to him. That was a hard thing for me to put my ugly stone on his holy shoulders, and when I did the weight caused blood to flow from his shoulders. I realized at that moment that Jesus is alive and real. Then, amazingly, the stone disappeared. Later, I read Ezekiel 36:26, "I will take out your stony hearts of sin and give you new hearts of flesh." God gave me a forgiving love for my friend—immediately. Since then, I continue to experience the freedom of the gift of the love and forgiveness of our Lord Jesus Christ.

—Jean Corbett, Rector's Assistant for
Pastoral Care (now retired), 1996

Author's note: Later, during a 2007 interview, Jean added that this "incredibly magnificent" vision began to liberate her from chronic, life-long shyness and resulted in public speaking. "After my life-changing encounter with Jesus, the healing of shyness was a process and at times was quite painful. This continued for several years—not instantaneous. When I met Jesus I promised him I would go or do whatever he asked me to do."

God Answers Prayer

I suffered from time to time with a severe back pain, making it difficult to move. I had one of these episodes when my father died. I wondered how I was going to get through all I had to do, what with family coming, etc. I asked some friends to pray for me.

During a Communion service, during which prayers were offered from me, the pain left completely. It usually took days or a week of resting. I know that God will heal and will enable me to do what has to be done if I trust Him and ask Him for help.

—Eve Evans, April 1996

Prayers for Safe Travel

Have you ever experienced any of the following incidents: hitting a dog that ran out in front of your car and grazing your bumper when you were traveling 70 miles an hour; your engine suddenly stops running when you were traveling 70 miles an hour in heavy traffic; or the hood of your car popping up in your face, shattering the windshield and blanketing your sight when you were traveling 55 miles an hour? I have had all these occur and I've survived them all, thanks be to God.

I usually pray for our safe travel, but sometimes I forget. It is such comfort to know that even if I take my eyes off of Him, He never takes His eyes off of me. He is always there for me whether I am aware at the time that I need Him or not.

—Marilyn M. Buist, June 1999

26

Eyesight Regained

A flicker of light, several rapid blinks, and all of a sudden something didn't work quite right in Billy Mitchell's field of vision.

That Sunday evening in 1986 seems like yesterday. He and his wife, Lil, were driving on I-85 back toward Simpsonville after visiting their son and daughter-in-law in Easley, South Carolina, when without warning Billy's left eye began to go. The sixty-year-old Navy retiree noticed that lights were bothering him. He remarked about this to his wife beside him in the passenger seat. "But there *aren't* any lights," responded Lil, bewildered.

The next day, while in the backyard cutting wood at his Simpsonville home, Billy observed the same visual phenomenon. By Wednesday the Mitchells were sitting in a doctor's office in Columbia, where the solemn words rang out, "You have almost 100 percent separation of the retina."

Quickly, Billy was admitted into the hospital for eye surgery. The following morning, the physician prayed with Billy before the operation. But a few days later there was disappointing news for everyone: "When he took the bandage off, all I could see was burnt orange. I could not see anything."

Ten days later (with his hand injured in a prior accident, unemployed, and without insurance), Billy faced yet another surgery at a hospital in Columbia. This time both eyes were bandaged for four days. Eventually, he also underwent laser surgery on the sightless eye. Good medical treatment all around, but to no avail.

"The doctor in Columbia said, 'There's absolutely nothing I can do to save this eye. It's gone.' He said that the lens and implants would not do any good. He said, 'I'm going to recommend that you wear a patch so that the bad eye will not compete with the good eye.'" Otherwise the right eye might also grow dim and lose sight.

Billy says the office exam declared his eyesight 20–2800, with 20–3000 being the technical benchmark for "legally blind." (Ideal vision reads 20–20.) "The only thing that I could see with that eye was just a burnt orange—nothing else."

Billy transferred his case to a Greenville physician closer to home, but his eyesight remained the same. He wore an eye patch for almost six years and eventually made peace with this turn of events—that is, until his sight was instantly brought back during a visitation by the Virgin Mary in 1992.

Pilgrimage Lifts the Veil

In the fall of that year an announcement was made at St. Elizabeth Ann Seton Catholic Church. There would be a bus trip to a notable place of Marian visitations near Conyers, Georgia. The group would leave from the Simpsonville church parking lot and arrive at the center in Conyers. Billy said, "Our Loving Mother was making appearances the 13th of each month. It was a pilgrimage and there were 42,000 people at that farm in Conyers. On that Tuesday the 13th there was a large number of people. We had a busload that had gone down there, people from different churches and areas."

He speaks of a defined eight-year period beginning in 1990 when apparitions of Mary were frequent—forty-nine in all—and adds that The Blessed Mother would convey a message on a regular basis through a spokesperson there.

Billy, Lil, and their adult daughter, Bonita, joined the bus pilgrimage several times. But during each trip, Billy was not in search of personal healing, although he did see stacks of discarded walkers and crutches from people who no longer needed them. "No, just going to worship and curiosity, mostly," he affirms.

Upon their first arrival, the Mitchell family was somewhat surprised at the large crowds. They walked around and explored. Although the two women were able to get into the actual Apparition Room, Billy could not because he had become separated from his wife and daughter and the area was jampacked with people. "This was a little house on the farm where the Blessed Mother was visibly making an appearance on the 13th of each month to a spokesperson," he says.

Billy says that day he heard a message relayed from The Blessed Mother that he still cherishes. "She said, 'As I depart today, many, many little flickering lights.' I was standing there at the chimney on the outside of the house. There were twinklings like Christmas lights. It was about one o'clock in the afternoon. They were just twinkling everywhere. I thought everybody saw them, but the more I talked to people, very few did see this. And this is something that occurred many times down there [at Conyers]. Different ones could see things. Others could not."

Lil and Billy decided to return to Conyers at a later date and get a more leisurely look. They did this the last Saturday of October 1992, the day he was healed. They sought out and walked parts of the grounds that were less crowded, careful to view statuettes and kneel at a special altar and cross. Next, they entered the Apparition Room, which Billy describes as a large, open space with several pews and two kneelers at the front. Lil knelt beside the wall, with her husband at the kneeler beside the fireplace.

And this is what happened:

"When I closed my eyes, the thing that I had always seen since my surgery (even with the patch on) was just a bright light. But now as I'm kneeling there—no particular prayer—I close my eyes, I cross myself, and I start to pray. I see this small object coming right towards me. It's burnt orange color. It's kind of weaving just a little bit as it's moving towards me and I open my eyes and I look at it again. I don't see anything. I close my eyes and immediately this little object continues to come straight to me. The patch was still on my eye.

"As this little object approaches, it looks like it comes right in and makes contact with my eye and when it does, my eye becomes black. The light's gone completely."

At this point, he removes the patch.

"I open my eyes, I look at my wife, and I can see her with my left eye. So after we finish our prayers, I'm stunned. I have no idea what's going on or anything else, I'm confused. We get up and we walk the grounds again."

He and Lil covered the Stations of the Cross. Other pilgrims did likewise. "The field where the Stations of the Cross are placed is quite large and surrounded almost in a circle with trees," says Billy.

He could still see everything just fine.

"And each time as we'd walk to a station I'd try to explain to my wife what I saw and what took place. I started to tell my wife and I got real excited, very emotional, and I told her I was able to see! I told her about the little object I had seen . . . that looked like it was a head, but there were no facial features. There looked like there were arms, but no fingers or hands. Two little feet, but like a cloak around them."

One can only imagine their joy. The Mitchells returned home in awe.

"I was blind but now I see," says John 9:25b (NIV).

Sunrise and New Day

When Billy got up from sleep the next morning and abruptly remembered the miracle, he felt a trajectory of emotion. Then he followed the habit of every single morning since losing his sight—"test the bad eye." He walked straight into the bathroom, gazed into the mirror, and covered each eye in turn. "And from the time I'd lost my eyesight in my left eye, I'd played games with it. I'd close my right eye and look to see if I could see anything. I'd done this many, many times. But that Sunday morning, when I opened my medicine cabinet and took this little bottle out, I put my hand over my right eye, and I could read the small print with my left eye."

Without hesitation, Billy made an eye appointment with his local specialist, now very familiar with his condition. The earliest available appointment was in less than two months. When the date arrived, Billy went to be assessed and the physician found a new reading of 20/60. The doctor was excited. "I'd gone from 20/2800 to 20/60. He wrote a prescription for a lens and said, 'Most people at your age start *losing* their vision.'" Only much later did Billy share with the doctor what had happened during the Conyers pilgrimage.

Billy drove directly from the eye appointment to an ice cream shop where Lil was working as a cake decorator. "Do you want the good news or the bad news first?" he asked.

Bad news first, Lil said, wanting to get it over with. The healing was real, but perhaps *sustained* healing was too good to be true?

So Billy hit her with this: "The bad news is, you're going to have to buy me a brand new pair of glasses!" He says she got all excited and started crying. "After that, it's been the same ever since. After that, I had no more eye problems."

Snapshot Captures Image in Sky

In yet another mystical sign, Billy was actually shown the image he had seen while on his knees in prayer the day of the healing.

About a month after Billy could see again with his left eye, he and Lil returned to Conyers with a group from St. Elizabeth Ann Seton Church. On the bus was a woman who had taken a photograph of the sky while visiting Conyers in October, the same month as Billy's healing. It clearly revealed the burnt orange, cloaked figure of a person. In it, Billy and others could easily trace the Blessed Virgin Mary's image.

He held up the photo during the interview for this story and beamed. "This is actually the picture she had. I think this looks like—and everybody there says—The Blessed Mother. . . . This is exactly what I saw that day."

Billy also displayed a letter from the Archbishop of Atlanta written in 1994 after the clergyman was provided "before" and "after" documentation about Billy's eye. The letter joined Billy in thanking God for the healing of the detached retina.

Billy says he doesn't flaunt his healing. He doesn't "grab" people to publicize his experiences. And yet, he will tell them unabashedly—if they only ask. He attributes his restored vision to "the healing power of Jesus Christ through the intercession of the Loving Mother."

A Divine grace of this magnitude sparks lifelong reflection and a desire for service.

"Now I'll tell you this—When I knelt on that kneeler, I was not praying for the return of my eyesight! I was not," says Billy. "I had just knelt down and the first thing I usually do like that is to thank God for his son Jesus Christ . . . I have conversations with Jesus. I don't get down and say all these fancy prayers . . . I thank him for all the blessings. Every single day we get blessings from God. My family has been blessed so many times. So many times, you can't even count the number of times we've been blessed, each and every individual in our family."

Lil says she agrees.

The day of the miracle, Billy had been at peace about his eye patch. He had long before accepted blindness in one eye and simply coped with it in daily life. So that day when he knelt to pray in the Apparition Room, all he planned to do was thank God.

"But I didn't even get a chance to do that! Because just as soon as I closed my eyes, I watched events start taking place. I didn't go down there to Conyers saying, 'I'm going to go pray for my eyesight, see if I can get my eyesight back.' I didn't do that. But I think in my heart that my wife probably was. . . ."

He chuckles and he smiles, a twinkle in both eyes.

"I have absolutely no problem calling the healing of the left eye at Conyers, Georgia, a miracle."

Author's note: Billy's family is featured in an earlier chapter. Following a naval career, he did industrial work and, most recently after receiving his sight, was employed in retail. Since the mid-1990s Billy has also cut grass at his church on a riding lawnmower because he wants to help in some way. He prays the rosary as he does so. He ushers on Sundays and spends extra time interceding with listed needs of the congregation and elsewhere. He has witnessed additional amazing acts of God, including dramatic healings through prayer.

27

Bodies, Spirits Made Whole

They are a small congregation. But as of January 2008, six physical healings and numerous signs and wonders just as life-changing have occurred on their watch. During a phone interview, Reverend Frank Seignious described two of these healings experienced at a growing non-denominational "church plant" that he and his wife, Charlotte, started in 2006. At first, people simply came together at the senior pastor's house. Then, from these modest beginnings, the group moved to a building. Now the small congregation has preliminary blueprints to construct a worship facility someday.

"Life Church of Charleston is a healing place. . . . Healing and praying for healing is a central part of what we teach every person to do. So from the very beginning, we have been praying for miracles. I always tell people, I don't heal anybody. I pray and the Lord Jesus heals," says Reverend Seignious. Many of the wonders have been in the realm of human relationships, resulting in powerful transformations. "Healing of broken relationships is as big a miracle as a physical healing. It just doesn't catch people's attention. But we're seeing that right now . . . our position is we want to do the things Jesus did. Two things that were normal in his life were healing and deliverance," says the pastor.

The first miracle that happens in a new congregation is always especially memorable, he explains. This initial event heightens faith and releases expectation. "That is always something that catches people's attention—when they see the impossible done by our Lord Jesus." He recalls that first super-natural healing miracle at their new church. "One of our members brought her eighty-seven-year-old mother to our 5 p.m. worship service on Sunday at our home. Her mother was quite a lady, with fiery red hair and a wonderful personality! She had not attended church in a while. She had a large bandage on the top of her left hand covering cancer which was scheduled for surgery. We prayed generally for her healing the first Sunday. The next Sunday, she told me she was going to have surgery on her hand that coming week. When the service ended, she remained seated in her chair in our living room. The other members went to our kitchen for refreshments. Charlotte and I walked over and explained we wanted to pray for Jesus to heal her. We were clear with her—we were praying for physical healing of her cancer. Typical of her . . ., she replied, 'Well, go ahead!' Charlotte and I knelt down. We simply prayed, 'in the name of Jesus and in the power of the Holy Spirit, be healed. Jesus cursed the fig tree and in Jesus' name we curse the cancer . . . and in His mighty name . . . we command you spirit and disease of cancer to wither and die. Your assignment against this woman is over. Come Holy Spirit, fill and renew her this day.' She left with her daughter and son-in-law around 6:30 p.m.

"Later that night, she called her daughter and said, 'You know, when I got home and took off my bandage—my hand really is a lot better. I don't think I will still need that operation.' The daughter, in her early sixties, responded immediately with, 'Mother . . . I know you don't want to have that operation. I am picking you up Wednesday at 10 for your 12 noon surgery.'" The older lady agreed.

The daughter drove her mother from her apartment complex to the operation. Reverend Seignious recalls their story: "When the surgeon came out and took off the bandage, he exclaimed in shock, 'What has happened to your hand? It is healed.' She replied, 'Well I know what happened. They prayed for healing at church and Jesus healed me.' The surgeon did not believe her story. He said, 'I want to see you in three weeks to see if this has held.' In three weeks, she said her hand was even better, and she just cancelled the appointment. This is our oldest member at the church. She is a living witness to the healing authority and power of Jesus."

As a greeting, each Sunday when this lady comes in, the pastor kisses her hand and invites others at the church to do so, saying, "Come kiss this lady's hand, because this was our first gift of miracles!"

A Heart Made Like New

A second supernatural intervention involved a middle-aged woman who came to the healing center. This "centerpiece" of the church's mission is open throughout the week and directed by Charlotte as the prayer healing minister, with intercessions for healing of body, soul, and spirit.

The woman in question had experienced a car accident and many infirmities. She had lost a very good job, and life in general had taken a tailspin, explains Reverend Seignious. "It was just a tragic story. She was so sick the left side of her heart was not working properly. She has other problems, too, but the thing that was just about 'doing her in' was her heart. She was so weak she couldn't even come to our worship service, so we told her to come to our home."

The Seignious couple sat with her for almost two hours. They underscored the biblical basis for healing, "showing her scriptures and preparing the room [spiritually], and binding up evil, and laying a foundation for the Lord Jesus to come, and then we told her that we were going to pray for her," says the pastor.

The cardiac operation was set for the next day, to be preceded by a heart catheterization to determine blockages. As the couple knelt beside her chair, recalls the pastor, "we began to pray against the heart disease. We began to pray in the mighty name of Jesus for full restoration. She went in the next day. They did the heart cath, and when she woke up, her doctor . . .

told her, 'When we got in we didn't have to do anything. There were no blockages and the left side of your heart is working normally. You have the heart of a twenty-one-year-old.' [She was either forty-eight or forty-nine.] And that was another huge sign of God's glory and authority. It is important for each disciple to be clear that we are called to pray—to pray for healing. But, we have to leave the results up to the Lord."

Seignious was ordained twenty-six years ago and spent almost all those years as an Episcopal priest. From the mid- to late 1980s, "God began to change my ministry by having it centered on prayer for healing," he says.

Day by day, it is a joy to see blessings rain down. He observes wholeness and abundant living as people assemble to pray. "When God gives you a healing, it's part of your witness. You have just been the recipient of his enormous grace."

Author's Note: In the early 1970s, Reverend Seignious graduated from USC School of Law with a J.D. degree and served as a criminal prosecutor with the 101st Airborne Division at Fort Campbell, Kentucky, in the office of the Staff Judge Advocate. Later, he attended Virginia Theological Seminary, where he received a master's degree in divinity.

While completing Miracles of South Carolina, I learned of a congregation in the Upstate that is experiencing supernatural outbreaks of this kind on a regular basis. Surely there are many such gatherings.

28

Tornado Lashes Lowcountry

On March 15, 2008, a tornado tore across Johnnie and Jean Corbett's 450-acre Bamberg tree farm. The storm toppled, uprooted, and splintered hundreds of trees. "The paths of destruction were all around us. It looked and smelled like the aftermath of Hurricane Hugo," emailed Jean. The Columbia Weather Service described area tornadoes that evening as "supercells" more typical of the plains states, say the Corbetts. The couple later learned that the rural town of Branchville three miles away lost century-old buildings, but lives were spared.

"Friday was a beautiful morning," recalls Jean. "We had a nice breakfast, then our morning Bible reading and prayers. As we closed our prayers, we asked the Lord to send angels to surround and protect our property here in Bamberg County and our home on Johns Island. This was a day to celebrate Johnnie's birthday with friends who were coming for the weekend (it was the opening of turkey season, too).

"That evening we sat on the porch overlooking the beautiful Cypress Swamp and Edisto River, with friends, guitar, banjo, and great singing. The next morning the hunters were up and out early calling turkeys, while the women and children slept in. One hunter bagged two turkeys midday. By late afternoon, everyone said their farewells. The sky was filling with dark rain clouds."

Johnnie adds, "The warm westerly breeze came through the open windows. When the last family left, Jean sensed a need to close the windows, even though the breeze was warm. After securing the windows, we sat on the back screened porch (facing the east) and happily recalled the events of the weekend with our dear friends. As we sat, the clouds began to produce lightning and thunderclaps. We laughed as a turkey in the swamp gobbled with every loud clap. Then, suddenly, a huge lightning bolt flashed across the river, followed by one of the loudest thunderclaps I ever heard. Jean jumped up, announcing, 'I'm going into the house!' I replied, 'I am, too.' We did, shutting the door behind us.

"Within minutes, the log house was pelted with hail and tree twigs. I watched from the south side as tall pines, majestic water oaks, and huge cypress trees bent in half, while some snapped or fell as the wind intensified. Jean watched the screaming wind hurl dark debris against the front windows. At that moment she realized it was a tornado, grabbed her purse, and yelled for me to get my wallet and 'let's get in the basement.' I got my wallet and continued to watch the trees. Jean stood frozen, staring at the terror that seemed to flex the closed windows. And then as quickly as the violent storm began, it was over.

"We were safe. The log house was safe," says Johnnie. "A contractor was staying in the little bunk house about one hundred feet away. I called out, 'John, are you okay?' The response was 'Yes!' The three of us quickly assessed the buildings and our trucks, car, and golf cart—no damage to our vehicles, no damage to the log house or the bunk house. The tornado(s) passed all around us and behind us, felling giant trees like toothpicks. A tree at least ninety feet tall fell across the ground-mounted electric power transformer, splitting it in half. Power poles were snapped, power lines down, and our only road out was blocked by trees that were impossible for us to remove."

Jean recalls this part of the story: "The Edisto Electric employees began cutting their way into our property about 3:30 a.m. They had to replace several power poles and re-string the wires. Those men are the equivalent to the cavalry riding up in their white trucks. I sat on the edge of my bed, watching flashlights moving down the road and listening to the sound of chainsaws, saying, 'Thank you, Lord, for those men and please keep them safe.' Friends began coming over the next day—Palm Sunday—cutting, dragging, burning trees and clearing paths for access to the farm buildings.

"The second day after the storm, Johnnie and our dear friend Rick Belser, retired rector of St. Michael's Episcopal Church in Charleston, went to the deep woods to survey the damage. They came up and I called from the porch, 'Well, Johnnie, how is it?' He replied, 'I have no words. Let Rick tell you.' Rick paused, and then with emotion said, 'When you see the full extent of the tornado damage all over the property, the clearer it is that God had his hand over this house. We're standing in the middle of a miracle.'

"That afternoon, we celebrated communion in our dining room looking out over the Cypress Swamp and fast-flowing Edisto River, with grateful hearts for the protection given us by our living Lord Jesus, while Edisto Electric lowered a new transformer from their truck."